C000098593

THE P _ _ _
IN YOU

A guided journey into your inner life
Finding your voice in poetry

First published by O Books, 2009
O Books is an imprint of John Hunt Publishing Ltd., The Bothy, Deershot Lodge, Park Lane, Ropley,
Hants, SO24 0BE, UK
office1@o-books.net
www.o-books.net

Distribution in:

UK and Europe
Orca Book Services
orders@orcabookservices.co.uk
Tel: 01202 665432 Fax: 01202 666219
Int. code (44)

USA and Canada
NBN
custserv@nbnbooks.com
Tel: 1 800 462 6420 Fax: 1 800 338 4550

Australia and New Zealand
Brumby Books
sales@brumbybooks.com.au
Tel: 61 3 9761 5535 Fax: 61 3 9761 7095

Far East (offices in Singapore, Thailand,
Hong Kong, Taiwan)
Pansing Distribution Pte Ltd
kemal@pansing.com
Tel: 65 6319 9939 Fax: 65 6462 5761

South Africa
Alternative Books
altbook@peterhyde.co.za
Tel: 021 555 4027 Fax: 021 447 1430

Text copyright Jay Ramsay 2008

Design: Stuart Davies

ISBN: 978 1 84694 025 5

A CIP catalogue record for this book is available
from the British Library.

Printed by Digital Book Print

O Books operates a distinctive and ethical publishing philosophy in
all areas of its business, from its global network of authors to
production and worldwide distribution.
This book is produced on FSC certified stock, within ISO14001
standards. The printer plants sufficient trees each year through
the Woodland Trust to absorb the level of emitted carbon in
its production.

THE POET
IN YOU

A guided journey into your inner life
Finding your voice in poetry

Jay Ramsay

BOOKS

Winchester, UK
Washington, USA

CONTENTS

for the inspiration we call poetry
for changing my life
and the lives of those I've loved & worked with

"But often, in the world's most crowded streets,
But often, in the din of strife,
There rises an unspeakable desire
After the knowledge of our buried life;
A thirst to spend our fire and restless force
In tracking out our true, original course;
A long to inquire Into the mystery of this heart which beats
So wild, so deep in us – to know
Whence our lives come and where they go"

– Matthew Arnold, *The Buried Life*

INVITATION

A poem is like a butterfly. A moment seeds itself inside us. A memory. An experience when we saw, we felt, perhaps even, we knew.

It touches deep in us. Deeper than words. And something begins, in that inner space. Something that is uniquely ours to speak of.

Creativity is naturally a process of incubation and birth. This book is designed to assist and guide you in this process.

It is an affirmative approach designed to respond to the needs of each individual person. It aims to honour and empower your own unique experience.

All you need is a commitment to yourself.

PREFACE

FROM CHRYSALIS TO BUTTERFLY

There is a poet in all of us. However unknown or neglected that part of us may be, it is there, often just waiting for the right conditions to present themselves.

Beyond writing poetry and being (and calling myself) a poet, I have known this since I realized that poetry is not just about literature and words on paper, it is alive in the living air all around us in any moment, and it is about our attitude to and relationship with life (all of life, and so it is also about death and dying).

Poetry is also about that primary voice in us that we can think of as the most radical part of who we are, belonging in our feelings and our individual authentic response to what happens to us and around us. That primary voice is something we all get educated and socialized out of (to a greater or lesser degree), indeed society would be impossible without these agreed terms of reference and description, however something is also lost in this process that Wordsworth referred to as "shades of the prison house", which was why Miroslav Holub, the Czech poet, spoke of poetry as being among "the first things of Man".

We may think of this in terms of dreams too, as well as play with its sense of expanse and experiment: in both the stirrings of our creative unconscious are free in a way they may later seem not to be.

Poetry is also about the imagination and gaining access to a different level of meaning. Nothing means anything merely at the concrete level beyond its function. That is materialism. For meaning, we have to get to another level which is symbolic, where things and events resonate with spirit. This is what the early 19th Century Romantics, Wordsworth, Coleridge, knew as Imagination (with a capital I). Through it, we can open to our lives as intrinsically meaningful as journeys of experience and development in time – that is, when we can find that primary voice, that basic experience of identity in us again. This is where the work begins.

If I don't know how I feel, I don't know who I am. What I have experienced working with groups and individuals again and again is the power of the imagination and the heart to restore us to what we feel and therefore who we are. The expression that comes as a result, through drawing and group sharing as well as in writing, is fundamentally healing, and may also involve the naming of something long held and never spoken.

Again and again I have seen faces lit up from within as a result of the writing that follows, and it is always a thread in the way I work in my private therapy practice.

The Greeks knew this as *catharsis*, for me – weird and suspect as it may be to the *Times Literary Supplement*-reading mainstream – it is living poetry where poetry and healing are about the same thing: that spark that makes us know who we are, the relief and wonder of being back inside the skin of things.

This book draws on material I have used in my one to one correspondence courses since September 1990. After the Introduction To Poetry which follows, there are nine chapters which offer a structured and experiential journey to and with 'the poet in you'.

Each chapter contains teaching in context, a suggested inner exercise, a writing exercise, and study poems and extracts, as well as some additional recommended reading – the whole course was originally designed to function over a nine month period of gestation. They can be taken more intensively, but the minimum period I would suggest would be nine weeks.

You can choose to work through this book on your own as solo work, and there is the option to correspond either with me as your tutor and guide, or one of the Chrysalis team (please see If You Wish To Work With A Tutor/Guide, as well as the Further Information section).

Either way, may it happen for you, and all the richness of your inner being come into expression where the poetry within you is waiting.

But first let's look more deeply at the roots and origin of poetry, and what that means for us in the climate of today.

INTRODUCTION TO POETRY

Hwaet !
A dream came to me
  at deep midnight
when humankind
  kept their beds
– the dream of dreams !
  I shall declare it.

The Dream of the Rood (10th Century)

The spirit world shuts not its gates,
Your heart is dead, your sense is shut
  — Goethe, *Faust* (19th Century)

Datta:
what have we given ?
  — TS Eliot, *The Waste Land* (1922)

INTRODUCTION TO POETRY

Poetry is an impulse as old as the human spirit: as old as language itself. We find it deep in time; in Isiah, Homer, St John, Corinthians (in the Bible), Dante, Shakespeare, Goethe – in writing and in names which have become myth and which have entered the stream of memory of our heritage and of our essence.

Poetry and the word 'poet' comes from the Greek *poesis*, meaning 'one who makes'. The poet, in relationship to words, is a maker of a special kind. In Latin, the word is *vates* meaning 'seer', diviner, or prophet. One who makes, and one who sees. These two meanings are at the root of what we are setting out to explore.

The definition of poetry is something primary; it is something that precedes the rational intellect. Poetry comes from the spirit, from inspiration.

Language is its tool. The mind is its mediator. Long before poetry was written down, and long before it began to be published as we know it, it was spoken aloud and learned by heart.

In our own Celtic past, this was the function of the bard. In Anglo-Saxon Britain, the earliest English poems we have would have been spoken in many different and slightly varying versions before they reached manuscript form. This would include *The Dream of the Rood* (just quoted on the previous page), as well as an epic like *Beowulf.*

The mediaeval figure of the minstrel, and in 12th Century France the troubadour, continued this oral tradition, a tradition that is still alive today in Macedonia, the former Yugoslav country bordering Greece, and in Russia, where poems of immense length are still memorized.

In Victorian and Edwardian England, and even more recently, people in school were learning poems by heart or by rote.

In connection with other and related cultures, poetry understood as something magical was deeply rooted in tribal feeling, and embodied in the shaman, the Bushman and the Aborigine, who by going intro a state of receptive trance brought back messages as well as healing from spirit.

Ancient priesthoods, such as the Ancient Egyptian, were imbued with ritual language – personified in the poet-pharaoh Akhnaton with his famous *Hymn to the Aten* (Sun), who transformed his country through its monotheistic inspiration.

Ezra Pound, TS Eliot's close friend and collaborator, referred to poetry as the wise language of the tribe.

We can see then that poetry, in its origin and essence, has clear preoccupations: the first is to speak truth, the second is to communicate that truth, and the third is to communicate it in language that sees, feels and dreams – in what ordinary or mechanical language is incapable of, in other words.

This is fundamental.

Poets are the sensitive antennae of their culture: of the place and time where they live. David Gascoyne, who became known as a young poet inspired by Surrealism in the 1930s, calls the poet a 'seismograph' – someone who experiences things not only personally, but collectively.

All art tells the story of its time – poetry, we can say, tells that story uniquely in words.

The history of poetry in any culture is bound up with storytelling in this sense – and it is in this sense we can understand it as a form of cultural divination.

Poetry divines the psyche of the culture it emerges in, and as poetry moves through time, the evolution of cultures in all their patterns of growth, decay, crisis, and rebirth.

Over time, poetry has emerged in different forms, each with different emphasis, named in periods (usually in retrospect). So during Renaissance England we have the 'Silver' court poets of the early 16th Century (the court of Henry VIII and Elizabeth I), the 'Metaphysical' poets of the mid-17th Century; then the 'Augustan' poets of the 18th Century, then the sudden brief revolutionary flowering of Romanticism after William Blake in the 1790s, before its slow dilution in Victorian times, and the disruptive reorientation of 19th Century poetry in both craft and content in 'Modernism' through Ezra Pound and TS Eliot in the early 20th Century.

The intellectual and academic status of poetry is something relatively recent, in so far as many people still feel the withdrawal of poetry as something accessible and comprehensible, reinforced in the way it has been taught. It is easy to forget that poetry was read as something seminal by large numbers of people, long before our age of television, DVDs and popular fiction.

Tennyson, the poet laureate of his time, was a best seller, and Byron's *Child Harold* sold out in London as soon as it was printed.

Our age places an emphasis more on the visual imagination.

Poetry is now more popular again than it has been for at least a century, even though publishers, especially the profit-driven ones, still mostly fail to recognize it.

Poetry has constantly been redefined across the breadth of human emotion and direction, and it has as constantly been defended, as far back as Sir Philip Sidney's text of 1519. Others have followed, notably through Romanticism, with its strongly value-orientated agenda. Samuel Taylor Coleridge wrote:

"The poet, described in ideal perfection, brings the whole soul of man into activity, with the subordination of its faculties to each other, according to their relative worth and dignity. He diffuses a tone and spirit of unity that blends and (as it were) fuses, each into each, by that synthetic and magical power to which we have exclusively appropriated the name of imagination."

– *Biographia Literaria*

Percy Bysshe Shelley was both more forthright and more simple in his Defence of Poetry in declaring poets to be the "unacknowledged legislators of mankind", and in his political poems he speaks to that spirit in the English people, both in his *Song to the Men of England* (sung for many years in working men's clubs), and in *The Mask of Anarchy*, written in rage after the terrible Peterloo massacre of 1819. There weren't many who thanked him for telling the truth about oppression. Poetic truth isn't any more comfortable than the teaching of the Gospels; and near the time of his untimely death (in 1822, aged only 29) Shelley numbered only 11 people he knew of who were actually reading his books.

In both Coleridge and Shelley's statements, you can hear the ancient echo of the consciousness I began by naming. The difference is that, centuries later, we find the poet in effect 'detribalized', and the advent of the outsider, named by existentialist philosophers and writers.

The relationship between poets and their society has always been tenuous and ambiguous because the best poets find themselves saying what their culture would rather not hear. Even in poets as relatively integrated into their society as John Dryden and in the 18th Century Alexander Pope, there is an awareness of this and an accompanying solitude.

The satirical emphasis which was magnified in his contemporary Jonathan Swift, famous for his Gulliver's Travels, drove Swift into madness. Swift's Gulliver remains, surrounded by a horde of Lilliputians only too eager to tie him down. And there is a Gulliver in all of us.

In more recent times, alienation in society and its lack of ecological relationship has been reflected in maladjustment – and in the suicidal deaths of poets such as Sylvia Plath and Harry Fainlight. More and more people are awakening to the price of distance and disconnection through a sensitivity which is, at root, poetry itself: its wellspring and source. And now we find ourselves in a time when contact with that source has become imperative, and not only for those of us who are poets – but, once again, for all of us.

So what is poetry? Or rather, what can we mean by it? There is a connection with prose (especially in Modern poetry), but the difference, apart from an obvious intensity and density of language, reflects on the function of poetry as heart-speech.

Poetry moves the heart where it reaches us and enters us, touching us at a level that is by definition deeper. All poetry aims to do this, whether it succeeds or not. But we know when it does – there is that distinct yet ineffable sense of our breath pausing, our eyes as if opened inwards, poised over the written form and movement among the lines, or where the poem ends, leaving us suddenly opened, quietly, blended with its feeling through each nuance of its word order and rhythm.

I remember vividly the first time I read Shelley's *Ode to the West Wind*, walking down by a Surrey river, down the hill from school. It was in a little battered leather Victorian edition I'd picked up for pence. Not so much to read as to have, and I found myself opening it as I stood near the water. It was an autumn afternoon, and the leaves had turned russet, glowing, and there was a breeze along the river and in the trees above it, enough to suggest wind that the leaves whispered to, hushing the air and suggesting a sense of anticipation at the same time.

My eyes moved into the poem, and immediately its rhythm held me, and as I read I was no longer aware of myself standing there, as the sound of the leaves blown by the wind began to move and the words glowed and caught fire, image after image drawing me through towards its ending. It was a moment out of time – we all have them – where the poem entered me and I entered it. It was a turning point, as I only later came to realize.

Something began in me that afternoon. I can say I was moved, but it was more than that. The feeling was of being called – of being addressed. I didn't know what it was, and I put the book away and walked on, finding myself seeing the river and the trees above it and the leaves in a way I hadn't before – or hadn't consciously. I wasn't looking at them, I was seeing them: I was seeing them alive. And they were calling too, and I was saying Yes – I say 'I', but it was also something else in me that was at the same time more familiar to me: utterly familiar, in fact. It was my own voice.

Poetry has to do with that unique voice we all have in us. It is not something we have generally been taught to believe, or give credence to. And this is something more than literature as we generally understand it. These are living words: not merely to be dissected or pinned like the wings of a butterfly.

We all speak a generalized language, defined by nationality and influenced by conditioning we are all molded by; and beneath that, spoken or unspoken, is another voice.

A door opens – and poetry can open that door into our own heart and towards our own truth, whatever it may be, and whatever it may need to sound like.

A door opens – and a journey begins. It is a call from the depth of us to be who we are. And it is the voice which can say, or begin to say, 'I am'. It is our birthright.

Poetry is a quest. At the same time, poetry is a response to the world – a response and an argument, both politically and spiritually, and particularly now the winds of change are blowing. We each need to have a vision of our time and what is happening in it and a sense of why it is happening.

By going more deeply into ourselves we are able to go more fully into the world and our relationships in it, with friends and strangers, seeing that we are all part of it. We are part of Creation and we are co-creators.

We find ourselves different from the world and its current values, and that is the dynamic of poetry. There is a cliche about poetry being 'unworldly' and this is the truth in it. We are in the world, but not of it (as St John says).

You could call this the outer calling. It is a calling to wake up, and to begin to see a way beyond the wasteland of nationality, prejudice, denial, exploitation and pollution; seeing a way too beyond these things in us and the unimaginative language we speak.

The poet inside us wakes and stirs, as the world stirs towards rebirth.

As George Trevelyan wrote in *Magic Casements*:

"In our over-masculinated society, in which logical analyzing intellect is used to gain our ends, the more feminine intuitive faculties are often allowed to go dormant. But these are precisely the faculties that make poetry. True imagination can blend with the being within form, and rediscover the miraculous oneness of all life. The poet is one who can crystallize into words this profound experience of identity."

We need space in order to write, and we need to learn to go inside and make a center there. Then it can begin.

There are as many ways to write a poem as there are people to write poems.

The contemporary scene (which is expanded on in the course which continues where this book ends) is a rich arena of diversity and difference. Poetry exists on many levels – light-hearted and serious, meditative and passionate.

It is wrong to start out by thinking there must be a 'right' way to write a poem. Poems often know more about themselves than we do, and the important thing is to let them come as they want to – in other words, to let yourself speak. Revision and rewording, if necessary, can come later. Another useful point to make here is to do with self-esteem (or the lack of it). Your poem, like your experience, need be no better or worse than anyone else's – it is yours. Comparisons are often unhelpful and de-energizing. We need to focus on and trust what we are trying to say. It is not an exam, and there is no certificate. It's much more challenging and more pleasurable than that – and there's no one here to mark you down.

There's no competition, either – and no prizes. We are the prize – and it's greater than anything we have so far imagined. And perhaps a little stranger, too.

CHAPTER 1

THE INNER POET

'He was a poet. He saw for our eyes and heard for our ears, and our silent words were upon His lips; and His fingers touched what we could not feel'

— Kahlil Gibran

THE INNER POET

* How can we begin to find the poet in us?
* Who is she or he?

That is the question we are going to begin by exploring. It is not so much a question to answer, it is more a question to hold, so you can begin to see what opens in you as a result.

Poetic identity is a tenuous and mysterious thing. Poets have always said so. If we go right back to the Anglo Saxon poet Caedmon, we find him describing in his poem the experience of being taken over and taken beyond himself; of going beyond his ordinary self-consciousness.

Something stronger than his ordinary self enters in and flows in the energy of the words he records. In a certain sense then, Caedmon the poet becomes the poet in the act of in this case speaking aloud his Song. He becomes someone 'other'. He becomes someone other, and yet at the same time he is himself, or rather more himself.

We have all had the experience of feeling of being more truly ourselves, and this can happen in many ways. We can experience this in thought, or in seeing someone else's face in thought. We may be out walking somewhere on our own. Or we may, unexpectedly, find ourselves glimpsing it as we look into a mirror. Who is this inner person, this inner being?

This is where it begins, whether we are aware of it or not. Arthur Rimbaud, the French 19th Century poet who wrote all his extant poems before the age of 19, coined the phrase, 'J'est un autre' ('I am another'). We can understand by this that he means 'I am something you cannot necessarily see', or even 'I am something you cannot see'.

More recently, the Russian poet Yevgeny Yevtushenko expresses this more concretely in the title of his collection *The Face*

Behind the Face. We might say the face behind the mask or the face behind the photograph.

We all have one. And it isn't necessarily a comfortable thing to realize, depending on what our relationship with this part of ourselves has been.

Equally, the recognition of it can be a joyous and liberating feeling a feeling of being able to breathe again. Or it may be a mixture of the two feelings, with others besides.

The face of the poet inside us may be hidden, but it cannot be masked. It is a naked face, a vulnerable, a 'feeling' face. It is a face that needs privacy and a face that needs protection. The problem with the protection, with the armour, is that it can become impenetrable, and then we are no longer really feeling, no longer really listening inside.

All poetry comes from a space of inner listening, and inner feeling.

And it is there we will begin to find the poet that is inside us, and the poet we each are uniquely and individually.

Visualization Exercise – Journey to Your Inner Poet

I'd like to suggest now that you do a simple exercise. You will need about ten minutes to do this, and a quiet and uninterrupted space in your day in which to do it best. You may want to take the phone off the hook before you begin.

Find a comfortable place to sit, and a comfortable position to sit or lie in; then gradually begin to turn your attention inwards. Be aware of your breathing, and allow your breathing to help you to turn inwards. As you do so, let go of your thoughts the thoughts you have been having, and the thoughts you have had reading this. Then close your eyes.

Begin to imagine a path in front of you. It may be a hazy image: don't worry. The path leads into a wood, in front of you, and you are walking on the path into the wood. You walk into the wood.

Be aware of what it is like. Be aware of the air, and of the trees, and the life there. You walk on, further in... and after a while, you begin to become aware that someone is walking beside you.

Be aware that this is your inner poet. Begin to see what he or she looks like, and of what your feelings are towards him or her. Has he or she anything to say to you? And do you have anything to say in return?

You might like to ask a question, or questions and see if he or she is willing to respond to them. Allow yourself time to do this. Don't hurry.

He or she may have a phrase or symbolic gift to give you as your dialogue ends.

As you receive the gift, thank him or her; and when you're ready begin to walk back, on your own, out of the wood.

Come gently back to yourself where you are; and feel your feet on the ground. Then open your eyes, and make notes on what you have experienced here.

You might want to doodle or draw; that can be helpful too. Try to retain as much of the experience as you can in detail. The smaller things are usually just as significant. They are all part of the picture.

You may want to discuss this experience with a partner or a friend; but images can lose their energy if they are talked about prematurely. It's worth being aware of this.

Over the weeks ahead, I would like to suggest you consider the following questions in connection with the visualisation on 'The Inner Poet' you have done:

i. What has been your relationship with this part of yourself in your life?

ii. What might it mean for you to have it more present?

You might like, or need, to reconnect to your memory of the figure in the wood as you consider these questions. You may anyway find the energy from the exercise continues to reverberate and connect up with other things in your perceptions. I would suggest you make some notes on this as well, and that as far as possible you trust and allow what comes.

One golden rule, that applies as much to dreams as it does to visualization work is: all the images are you.

Keeping a journal can be very useful here, as it is a way of tracing the development of a process; in this case your own creative process, and the way it connects to things and events in your life.

To write is to remember. All writing, in this sense is a remembering; a bringing together that nourishes and extends our awareness.

We will begin to explore writing itself, in your own poems, in Chapter 3. Next chapter, we will be locating the voice that poems are made of. For now I would like to leave you reflecting on 'The Inner Poet' with two study poems, chosen in this context; and invite you to be aware of the language and feeling in both of them, and where, as poems, they are 'coming from'.

Study Poems

The first poem, by William Blake, was written c.1790 as part of his *Songs of Experience*, which he illustrated with his own engravings.

The poem captures a particular clarity, and is spoken with a particular authority.

'Bard', with its Druid overtones, means 'poet'. The bard here is also a figure of guidance.

The second poem, by American poet e.e.cummings (who chose to spell his name deliberately in lower casement lettering) was written in the 1930s. His poetry is marked by an ability to experiment with language and the layout of words and lines, in a fresh and innovative way. It is a poem about intimacy with a companion and about what it means to speak from the heart.

THE VOICE OF THE ANCIENT BARD

by William Blake

Youth of delight, come hither,
And see the opening morn,
Image of truth newborn.
Doubt is fled, and clouds of reason,
Dark disputes and artful teasing.
Folly is an endless maze,
Tangled roots perplex her ways.
How many have fallen there!
They stumble all night over bones of the dead,
and feel they know not what but care,
And wish to lead others, when they should be led.

('SOMEWHERE I HAVE NEVER TRAVELLED')

by e.e.cummings

Somewhere I have never travelled, gladly beyond
any experience, your eyes have their silence:
in your most frail gesture are things which enclose me,
or which I cannot touch because they are too near.

Your slightest look easily will unclose me
though I have closed myself as fingers,
you open always petal by petal myself as Spring opens
(touching skilfully, mysteriously) her first rose

or if your wish be to close me, I and
my life will shut very beautifully, suddenly,

as when the heart of this flower imagines
the snow carefully everywhere descending;

nothing which we are to perceive in this world equals
the power of your intense fragility: whose texture
compels me with the colour of its countries,
rendering death and forever with each breathing.

(I do not know what it is about you that closes
and opens; only something in me understands
the voice of your eyes is deeper than all roses)
nobody, not even the rain, has such small hands.

Suggested reading

William Blake *Songs of Innocence & Experience*, and his poem *'Auguries of Innocence'*.

e.e.cummings Selected Poems (Faber & Faber).

Your favourite poems: re-reading them, if you have them.

David Malouf *An Imaginary Life* (Picador), a short and very special novel, about the poet Ovid's meeting with his guide who is a wild boy.

Please also note the references for the Introduction to Poetry, listed at the end of this book.

Suggested reading from these, over the duration of this book, would include The Earliest English Poems, T.S.Eliot's *'The Wasteland'*, and George Trevelyan's *Magic Casements* - a personal anthology of poems with his own illuminating commentary, if you can locate it. (Co venture, 1982).

I would also recommend the new *Penguin Book of English Verse* edited by Paul Keegan (Penguin, 2001), a wonderful overview of centuries of poetry, presented chronologically, which also includes many women previously ommitted – as well as Irish poets.

CHAPTER 2

LOCATING THE INNER VOICE

'What, in the last analysis, induces a man to choose his own way and so climb out of unconscious identity with the mass as out of a fog bank... it is what is called 'vocation'. Who has vocation hears the voice of the inner man; he is called... to have vocation means in the original sense to be addressed by a voice.'

— C.G. Jung

LOCATING THE INNER VOICE

All poems are voices. Poems are made of language, of words that are recorded in particular combinations of meaning and rhythm: and the essence of those words, whatever the kind of poem, comes from the voice and is 'uttered', is spoken.

In this sense, we can remember that speech comes before written language; poetry was spoken long before it was written down. It is, at root, an oral art. And yet clearly the voice of a poem is different from our normal speaking voices; and the difference is what we are looking at here in this chapter.

The poetic voice is an inner voice, an inner whispering that is simultaneously spoken and silent. It is a voice that is individual to each of us (and individual to each poem as well). It's interesting to reflect on Jung's remarks about 'vocation' in this sense, quoted above at the start of this chapter; and that, as he says, the root meaning or etymology of the word means 'to be addressed by a voice'.

Some people describe poetry as 'a calling', but you can see how describing poetry as a 'vocation' is actually more precise.

We have all had the experience of taking down dictation. Writing a poem is similar, the difference being that firstly, it is a voice coming from inside; and secondly, it is a voice which is in the process of speaking, and in all its pauses and hesitations as well as its fluency is a voice that is searching for words for itself. It is a voice that is searching for words for itself in the act of speaking. And we listen, and we are hearing words and we are searching for them.

Ordinary speech is less conscious in this respect: less deliberate. We speak more quickly. And there is poetry in what we speak, and we are often unaware of it.

We may be more aware of it when we are finding it harder to find words or when we are moved by something. Sometimes you can hear the quality of your voice changing then.

Suddenly and subtly, it has a richer resonance. We may even be aware that our level of quality of expression has changed, as well even in the odd sentence or turn of phrase.

We may even say to ourselves afterwards 'I wish I'd written that down' or 'It's funny how when you have the best conversations there's never a recorder handy'.

What were we saying? There were words, and they had a particular feeling to them, a rightness, a depth and that can relate to any emotion: anger, or nostalgia, sadness or wondering.

Poetry is first and foremost something spoken; and for many people, poetry is something they are 'saying' before they begin 'writing' it.

The other thing is this: we can say at such moments that voice is my own. 'My own', not in the sense that I possess it, but in the sense that it is authentic. Think how often we speak, how often we are making our voice heard and yet how often is that voice really ours? It may sound like it; but the difference here is that the voice has substance. We are saying something. We are speaking our truth and speaking it feelingly. This also means we are saying it in our own way.

We all know this voice, and it is often a voice we have neither been credited with nor encouraged to have. In many people this voice is effectively gagged; either as a result of negative experience or fear and embarrassment or both. We all speak a conditioned language to a greater or lesser extent. This is inevitable. If we all spoke an utterly private language, society would be impossible.

At the same time, part of our voice gets left out. In political terms, this may be active suppression. The real voice is pushed down because it is too threatening. We can do this to ourselves, too. And the price is slavery and illness literally, *dis-ease*.

Poetry, in this sense, is unconventional anarchic, even. It is what we don't say, or are unable to fully say out loud. And of course it is more than this as well.

Poetry is unexpected, it is inspiration: literally, breathed speech or the speech of breath.

Traditionally, it's related to the muse: meaning the feminine or receptive part of ourselves, also the part that is capable of being and listening.

Classically, three of the Nine Muses were muses of poetry the others were connected to water and to memory both states of receptivity, both elements of what you could simply call 'soul', and both vital elements to the poet in us.

Poetry means to find that voice; and poems are records of finding. And so to be, and begin to be, a poet means finding your own voice not someone else's, but your own.

There are many kinds of poet, but for the sake of emphasis here I want to say there are two kinds: the first who learns to write poems through reading other people's, and often copying or imitating other poets; and the second who learns to write from listening to his or her own voice.

Of course all poets learn from other poets, and poets can be positively influenced by other poets. This has mainly to do with style and technique.

But the voice we are speaking of here is something primary. And the poetic voice is not primarily of the mind (though it uses the mind) but of the intuition, or intuitive mind the mind that exists at all the levels of our being: head, heart and body.

It is different for each of us, and perhaps different for women and men. For some, it's like when we say it's from the gut, the belly; for others, the experience of the inner voice can be more like a haunting, even a feeling of being 'spoken through'. For others, it's the heart. It depends. But in every case, the voice is something in you and is something that is also physical, just as you are.

Exercise: Finding Your Inner Voice

I'd like now to suggest another exercise to help you locate your inner voice. Again, you will need ten or fifteen minutes to do this, and a quite space to do it in. Read this carefully right through before you begin: and have your writing things handy.

Lie down flat on the floor, on your back, with your eyes closed. Again, be aware of your breathing, and take a few deep breaths to relax your body, relaxing a little more with each breath. Be aware you are going to locate your inner voice.

As you lie quietly relaxed, be conscious of your body; of what you are lying in.

And then, start to feel the energy of your inner voice; and begin to get a sense where the energy is coming from or where it is entering you.

Include any thoughts your mind may have, and if you can, let them go.

Let go to the awareness you are having of this energy.

It may be in your legs. It may be in your belly... or your hands... or your head feel the energy of your voice, and let it build. Don't worry about words or speech: let it build.

If you are having any difficulty, just keep breathing; and feel your breath holding you.

Then when you are feeling the energy clearly enough for yourself, gradually let it begin to come into your throat. Let it come into your throat, and then out out through your mouth.

It may be just sounds, or a sound. It may be words. Try not to censor it. Stay with the energy, and let it be what it is. Keep breathing.

Begin to listen to the voice, and if you can, welcome it. Let it be there as it is, without judgement. Just allow the sounds, or the words to come. If there are words, be aware of them. If there are sounds, be aware of how they are sounding. Let your throat sound, and your mouth move as it wants to.

Then gradually begin to let the energy die down, but to the

part of your body it started in and came through. Let your voice die down, and return.

And then lie quietly for a while, lie still. You may want to stretch then.

Open your eyes, and slowly get up. Don't hurry this. You may feel a little dizzy.

Then make some notes on your experience here and what happened.

You may find if you choose to repeat this exercise that the inner voices comes from a different part of you; and that's fine. Just be aware of the energy, as before, and try and allow your self to go with it.

As you make notes on your experience, be aware also of what gender the voice is for you. It may be either. And again, try and note your experience in full.

As Cicely Berry says: 'The primary object then it is to open up the possibilities of the voice...', and this exercise is designed as a loosening. Whatever happens to you here is right. Whatever happens to us always reflects where we are, whether we like it or not. Whatever happens is ours, and understood rightly, that is always a consolation.

Remembering your thoughts and feelings in connection with this experience, I would like to suggest these questions to you:

i. What is it like to listen to this voice of yours?
ii. How free do you feel your voice has been in your life?
iii. How able have you been to say what you mean?

You may want to reflect on this in your journal; or if you have done so already, look up the relevant entries. Next chapter, we are going to begin to bring your voice into writing.

Include your feelings about this, remembering that they are part of a process and that they can change. Or as Starhawk once said 'Where there is fear, there is power'.

Study Poems

The study poems that follow are all on the theme of the inner voice the voice that poems are made of, and which we are called on to express.

They are all about the experience and the truth of this.

The first poem, by Thomas Hardy was written in December 1912. It is one of several poems he wrote after the death of his wife that left him with feelings of remorse, facing the unknown. The 'airblue gown' refers to her dress; and 'wistlessness' here means a state of unknown being ('wist' is archaic for 'known').

The poem by Russian poet Anna Akhmatova, written in 1924, speaks beautifully and amusingly for itself.

The poem by contemporary poet and a feminist Michele Roberts (published in 1986) may reevoke also your experience with 'The Inner Poet'. Michele Roberts evokes the journey to the voice, in the sense of authentic self-expression. It is a journey that begins with heroism, and which turns, in the event, into real humanness a humanness which includes humility. The last lines are important here.

I would invite you to reflect on the theme of the voice and of 'guidance' in these.

Suggested reading follows, and references and bibliography are found at the back of the book.

THE VOICE

by Thomas Hardy

Woman much missed, how you call to me, call to me,
Saying that now you are not as you were

When you had changed from the one who was all to me,
But as at first, when our day was fair.

Can it be you that I hear? Let me view you, then,
Standing as when I drew near to the town
Where you would wait for me: yes, as I knew you then,
Even to the original airblue gown!

Or is it only the breeze, in its listlessness
Travelling across the wet mead to me here,
You being ever dissolved to wan wistlessness,
Heard no more again far or near?

Thus I; faltering forward,
Leaves around me falling,
Wind oozing thin through the thorn from norward,
And the woman calling.

THE MUSE

by Anna Akhmatova, translated by Richard McKane

In the night when I wait for her to come
life seems to hang on a strand of hair.
what are honours, what is youth, what is freedom
before the dear guest with the little flute in her hand?

There, she has entered. She threw back her veil
and looked at me inquisitively.
I ask her: 'Was it you who dictated
to Dante the pages of Inferno?' She answers: 'It was I.'

THE WOMAN WHO WANTED TO
BE A HERO

by Michéle Roberts

the first task was to persuade them
a woman could go
that my heart could and did ring
like warrior drums
that I could curtsey to dragons
and then slay them
that I could leap seven leagues
at the drop of a highheeled boot
my mother and father complained
there was no farewell ritual for me
but I had brandnew disguises

the second task was to search
in a dark wood for years
alone, and afraid, and not knowing
whether I touched
men, or gnarled trees, or hobgoblins
still, I learned songs, and the way of the wild
and the wise witch showed me
the way out of the wood

the third and hardest task
is letting you search for me
through thorns, over glasstopped walls
past siren music
and the sleepy drugs of flowers
I must stand still, I must wait
wet, humming aloud, smelling
sweet, smelling strong

certainly, I have few words
and no tricks
for this

Suggested reading

William Wordsworth *The Prelude* (Penguin).

It's a huge poem, and I suggest that you dot about in it. It's about the birth of the poet in him, through his experience with Nature in his native Lake District.

Percy Bysshe Shelley's Poems *'Ode To A Skylark'*, and *'Ode To The West Wind'*.

Both are poems which uniquely evoke the poetic voice. Faber publish a selection of Shelley; Oxford University Press publish his complete Poetical Works.

Other Hardy poems, if they strike you, from his Poems of 1912-13.

Michéle Roberts, as above.

Poems you have already have and read; being aware of them as 'voices'. (some of your own poetry as well).

CHAPTER 3

INTO THE HEART

And the future will be nothing less
Than the flowering of our inwardness.

— Rainer Maria Rilke

INTO THE HEART

Feeling of a special kind is something basic to poetry of all kinds. It is this quality which distinguishes it from other forms of language, and it is this quality which makes it memorable.

A poem is a voice that speaks in feeling; and a poet is someone who has an unusual capacity for feeling. It's the part of us that feels.

What is this feeling? and what does this capacity to feel mean? To be clear about this, we need to make a distinction which to some people is obvious, and to others, less so: it is between feeling on the one hand, and emotion on the other. We are emotional beings: up and down, angry and sad, ecstatic and frustrated but feeling, though connected, is something different. It is something finer, and often less overt as well. It is the difference between the solar plexus and the heart.

William Arkle, a visionary painter and thinker who died in 2000, likened the difference to music. Where emotion is often something extrovert or 'full blast', like a brass band, feeling (and the heart) is more like a string quartet... as he said 'so small sometimes we hardly know it is there'. The difference is also easy to reflect on if we take the stock phrase 'a man of feeling', and compare it with 'a man of emotion'.

This isn't to negate emotion; rather to clear space for it so it can become something else, something that may surprise us when we find ourselves writing out of an emotional experience or memory.

Emotion grinds the grain; the heart separates the wheat from the chaff. Sometimes this process takes place within a poem — there are examples. This is a process that is anyway going on inside us in our daily lives when we say we are 'working through something' often something which has caused us difficulty or hurt, or even incomprehension.

Poetry is born out of a synthesis of heart and mind, out of what we can call 'heart-mindfulness'. Experience becomes feeling, a feeling which suffuses the language we have at our disposal through the mind's resources.

But in the moment of writing, what is it that speaks? (or what is it that largely speaks?) when we are no longer aware of ourselves as we usually are and the words begin to warm and flow almost in spite of us.

It is the heart. It is the heart that catches the wind like a sail raised on a boat; it is the heart that breathes and expands as it speaks. And the heart is something vast: as small as a wren and as broad as a sunset. It is something we find, or come to find ourselves in.

Pascal wrote in his *Pensées*: 'The heart has its reasons that Reason does not know'; and tradition has it that the 13th Century Sufi poet Jalaludin Rumi, who was a well-known scholar, was sitting by the river one day reading when a wild eyed fakir (or holy man) came up to him, picked up his books, and threw them in the fountain, telling him in no uncertain terms that he would never find what he was looking for there. 'You'll only get it from here', the fakir said, striking himself on the chest, and at that moment, Rumi was seized with feeling feeling that resonates through all his poems, in their clear, powerful poised gentleness. Pascal's own experience, which led him (a philosopher) to almost inarticulately repeat the word 'fire', was one which he wrote on a small piece of paper, folding it and sealing it in a locket which he wore till the end of his life.

We have all had such experiences, and we don't have to be saints or philosophers to have them. Whether we are open to them or not is another question or, perhaps, the question. We can all trace, or begin to trace, the thread of our hearts in our lives, seeing life as it is as a journey in feeling that is our birthright as human beings, and who knows, maybe no one can take that away from us, only ourselves. So it is a thread that may seem to be lost, but which in reality never is because it is us, wherever we are sitting or walking or standing.

John Keats called this 'the holiness of the heart's affection'. It is affection and it is passion. It is a kind of fire. It is the fire that led Dylan Thomas to write the line 'And death shall have no dominion'; and which led Liverpool poet Brian Patten to echo him in his 'And doubt shall not make an end of you'.

It is an energy we can feel also in the other elements of water, earth and air: all of which are part of the heart and its feeling-variation, naturally blending and interfusing, and mirrored in our own wordless feelings and in what we find to be our vocabulary of feeling.

It's no accident, then, that some of us are 'fiery', some 'watery', others 'airy' or 'earthy'; we all have our own particular emphasis, our own depth and subtlety of being.

Poems mirror their authors in this way and so poems come physically (in this sense) from us; and we can find out a lot more about who we are by writing them.

We have all been taught to look out into the world: we have been taught a lot less about looking in to ourselves, and in to the world. We are invisible, even 'unfeeling' towards ourselves and so the world is, tragically, invisible to us.

The heart knows this, which is why it never leaves us alone; or not for long. It may even have to resort to desperate strategies to gain our attention. And the heart has this purpose in all of us to bring us to who we really are. The heart is the ultimate realist. And remember Pascal.

We can see the heart, then, as a thread or 'heartline' in our lives, illuminating certain experiences and moments which we can think of as being 'inspired' (or literally, 'breathed'). And we can see that the heart itself sees and it is this seeing that is essential to poetry, to poetic seeing: to what it means to see something, or a situation, with more than just the eyes and more than just the mind. It means we are seeing feelingly, or seeing with our heart through our eyes seeing in a way that certain things inspire or compel us to. And this may be in the present or it may be as a result of something remembered, but the feeling is the same and we want and need to begin to express it.

We can talk about it, which means expressing it outwardly (which we often do); a poem requires that we take it inward, that we speak in inwardly. As I said in the last chapter, there is a connection and a difference between the two.

The voice we all have is something deeply rooted in us, more deeply than we often know. It is already there. It is not something we have to acquire. To speak from our feelings may require courage or trust trust in the mystery but as we do we find an answering energy or impetus that has a quality both of clarity and even forthrightness. It needs to be said 'this way'. Or as poets have often effectively said through their poems 'these were the words to say it'.

We find words but equally, words find us. This is important. May people think they can't write because they have to find the words. They often haven't thought that it is mabybe a question of letting the words find them. What does this mean? It means with all the determination and the knowledge of words there is we also have to let go. To let speak.

I offer this to you as I believe it is the key.

Exercise: Writing from the Heart

I'd like now to suggest this exercise for going into your heart and this time, writing from it. Again, it may be useful for you to have your writing things to hand, and for you to read this once or twice through so you are clear about what you are doing so you can allow whatever needs to happen to take place.

Find yourself a comfortable position in which you feel relaxed and at ease, including what you may be feeling. Allow it. Close your eyes and take a few slow deep breaths, breathing in energy and calmness, and breathing out any stress or resistance you may be experiencing.

When you are settled in yourself, start to reconnect to the figure of your inner poet in whatever way seems most appropriate to you. As you focus on it, you will know.

Then, remember the experience and the energy of your inner voice, and reattune to it. Be aware of its resonance and timbre and of how it feels.

Now, loosely holding the experience of both... find yourself walking down a road. Again, be aware of what it looks like and of your surroundings. Keep walking.

Eventually, you come to a crossroads, and at the crossroads there is a signpost.

One road leads to sadness; the other road leads to joy. Pause for a moment, and decide which road you want to walk down first.

Then start your journey down the road to a sad or joyful experience you have had in your life which has moved your heart. Be aware of the details on the road as you walk towards it notice the colours, the people, the things, the atmosphere as you closen... then arrive.

You arrive at a place where the incident is reoccurring for you. Watch what is happening. Notice each detail. Really see what is taking place, and as you do so, see what you are feeling, and allow yourself to feel it. Let the feeling permeate your awareness and your being. What is its essence? As you ask yourself, see what comes to you. You may already be seeing it, but if you are unsure, then ask again. Let it come.

When you feel you have seen enough, turn round from where you are standing or sitting and walk back up the road you have travelled to the crossroads. Again, pause there, and taking your pen or biro, make some brief notes (you may also want to draw or doodle). Stay with the feeling.

Then, when you're ready, close your eyes again and take the other road.

Again, walk down it being aware of what is with and around you as you come to the place where you find yourself re-experiencing this sad or joyful incident. Again, let yourself re-experience it in feeling holding the same question.

Then walk back up to the crossroads, taking your time; and make some more brief notes. Then, finally, walk on from the crossroads straight ahead down the 'road of now' towards yourself where you are... and slowly come fully back into your room. Don't rush. Stay with the feeling.

Add to your notes, if you need to. Then choose which experience you wish to write about first. Stay with your notes, taking a separate sheet of paper (or a typewriter if you want to write straight onto one); and start to see what wants to come in words. Try and let the words come as they want to and try not to edit or question them as they do. If you write into the feeling, you will find a pattern for them will begin to emerge, however roughly; and groups of lines will occur.

Follow the feeling, and let it gain strength and direction. Keep following it. You will find that it moves towards an ending, even if the feeling itself remains unfinished.

The words will suggest an ending. You may feel you have left something, or some words out. Make a note of them or of the sense of them. Remember: this is a draft you are making.

When you have completed the first as far as you can, turn to the second.

You may want to go straight on to the second, or stay with the first for a while.

Try and see what your poem needs from you in either case by way of attention.

If the energy is still with the first of your poems, stay with it.

If you are having difficulty, go back to the crossroads where you made the original notes, and reconnect to the feeling there. The original feeling is the source that is worth remembering, particularly if you feel you are 'going away from it' in a way that feels false or inauthentic to you. And don't worry about the language at this stage. There's no one judging you.

The important thing is that you are beginning to write; and that a journey of any length begins with the first step. And the first step can seem huge and there's a sense in which every time we write, it's like the first time.

That feeling is so much part of the experience of writing a poem, and is (I think) necessary to it; necessary if the poem is to occur in its own free space, its own often surprising space. So it is like taking a step or a jump. And at the same time, we are safe on the ground. It happens again and again.

Give yourself time to work on these. It may be you work quickly or slowly the pace is yours, and there is no right or wrong. If you feel yourself tiring beyond a certain point, then stop with the intention of continuing. And certain times of day may be better than others for you to work on this: first thing in the morning, or evening, or late at night.

It's best not to talk about what you're writing while you're writing it. The energy disperses and it comes away from your centre. Some people are more sensitive to this than others.

But this kind of energy is often more fragile than it seems, as we often become aware when it has apparently slipped away unnoticed. And then it can be difficult to retrieve.

So keep at it. You may want to make several attempts at either or both poems, as long as the energy stays with them, and in you. Or other apparently unconnected ideas to write from may come to mind.

Be open to them! And don't feel bound to the exercise. It is an evocation, that is all. Your experience is what matters as a result of it above and beyond it.

Study Poems

The study poems that follow are all round the theme of the heart and the feeling we have been exploring here. I have chosen examples which reflect both roads, relating to passion and joyousness, sadness and woundedness. Each of these four poems speaks powerfully in its feeling, and I would invite you to read and consider them in this way.

The first poem (untitled) by Emily Dickinson was written in the 1860s, as one of over a thousand poems that were largely unpublished in her lifetime. She lived a life of intense retreat at Amherst, near Boston, and developed a style that (like that of Gerard Manley Hopkins) was entirely her own. Hers is a passion poem that goes straight into the feeling as its height and in its essence with its metaphor of surrender in 'Compass' and 'Chart', which represent the mind. It is a poem of passionate return, to the heart, to sexuality, to the source.

The second, by D.H.Lawrence, is connected in feeling and was written c.1912 soon after he married Frieda. It is one of his most joyous and prophetic poems, and one which speaks powerfully to our time. It is a poem about the heart's wind, and about being a channel to it and it echoes the 'forthrightness' I mentioned in its striking simplicity of phrasing and its long outriding lines. It is a poem that 'breathes out' as you can see. And what of the 'three strange angels'? They are what we fear most that will both welcome and give us the most.

When I first read the third poem, by W.H.Davies, it was the kind of poem I wanted to see copied and posted through everyone's door. Davies, who was 'discovered' by George Bernard Shaw was an uneducated genius of feeling who lived a considerable part of his life as a tramp or 'gentleman of the road'. And he knew the road: he slept under hedges, and felt the cold, and the sun and the rain on his face. Later (by 1922) he was 'indoors', but he had far too much humility to ever become respectable or bourgeois. His poem speaks for itself and himself.

Fourth and last is a poem by the contemporary poet Elaine Randell (published in 1988) which, as simply, is a plea for us to see with our hearts and see how the heart makes oneness between all living things. Here again, you can see how the tone of the poem blends from line to line in its meaning and the gesture it is making. It is a cry from the heart and from the soul.

You might find it useful (as well as enjoyable) to read these poems aloud to fully get their flavour and feeling; and if you do, notice the difference in how you feel after you've read them out. You might also like to get a friend to read them to you. Enjoy them and yourself, as you do.

WILD NIGHTS

by Emily Dickinson

Wild Nights — Wild Nights!
Were I with thee
Wild Nights should be
Our luxury!

Futile — the Winds —
To a Heart in port —
Done with the Compass —
Done with the Chart!

Rowing in Eden —
Ah, the Sea!
Might I but moor — Tonight —
In Thee!

SONG OF A MAN WHO HAS COME THROUGH

by D.H.Lawrence

Not I, not I, but the wind that blows through me!
A fine wind is blowing the new direction of Time.
If only I let it bear me, carry me, if only it carry me!
If only I am sensitive, subtle, oh, delicate, a winged gift!
If only, most lovely of all, I yield myself and am borrowed
By the fine, fine wind that takes its course through the chaos of
       the world.

Like a fine, an exquisite chisel, a wedgeblade inserted;
If only I am keen and hard like the sheer tip of a wedge
Driven by invisible blows,
The rock will split, we shall come at the wonder, we shall find
       the Hesperides.

Oh, for the wonder that bubbles into my soul,
I would be a good fountain, a good well-head,
Would blur no whisper, spoil no expression.

What is the knocking?
What is the knocking at the door in the night?
It is somebody wants to do us harm.

No, no, it is the three strange angels.
Admit them, admit them.

THE DUMB WORLD

by W.H.Davies

I cannot see the short, white curls
Upon the forehead of an Ox,
But what I see them dripping with
That poor thing's blood, and hear the axe;
When I see calves and lambs, I see
Them led to death; I see no bird
Or rabbit cross the open field
But what a sudden shot is heard;
A shout that tells me men aim true,
For death or wound, doth chill me through.

The shot that kills a hare or bird
Doth pass through me; I feel the wound
When those poor things find peace in death,
And when I hear no more that sound.
These catlike men do hate to see
Small lives in happy motion; I
Would almost rather hide my face
From Nature than pass these men by;
And rather see a battle than
A dumb thing near a drunken man.

"TELL THEM HOW EASY LOVE IS"

by Elaine Randell

How the light mist comes up and across
the marsh in late afternoon
how the big trees are so big.

If I was a man the love of a good woman
would keep me safe and wear me out.
Tiny flowers in the wood tonight
I picked a few and brought them home.
Crow and sheep share the same water trough
Just the way the light rises
up drawing together the day and the voices
of the people warm in their homes.
O tell them how easy love is.

* Suggested reading

Rumi's poems. There are a number of translations of this remarkable enlightened poet.

Coleman Barks (as above); also translations by Robert Bly, Daniel Liebert, and Andrew Harvey.

W.H.Davies Collected Poems (Oxford University Press).

Kenneth Patchen Love Poems - Patchen's poems are marked by their lyrical naturalness and directness of expression, with rhythms aligned to jazz; he was a major influence on Beat Poets like Allen Ginsberg in the 1960's.

Two contemporaries: Owen Davis *I+I* and Elaine Randell *Beyond All Other*.

There is also the film about Jung called *A Matter of Heart*, available on DVD, which is relevant in every respect.

CHAPTER 4

THINGS

'All values must remain vulnerable, and those that do not are dead'

— Gaston Bachelard

THINGS

All poems are things, and things give rise to poems.

A poem, as we know, is 'about something'; and poems in this sense are the most intimate record of our experience of what happens to us in relationship to our world.

We say suchandsuch a thing happened, as a result of which I wrote this. Or it was 'the thing about' a person, an event or an object that made it special, that made it specific to us.

It wasn't just any tree, it was this tree. This flight of swifts. This stone.

Again, we need to begin by making a distinction that is often blurred: and that is between an *object* and a *thing*. The difference is our presence in relationship to something (this stone, say); and a quality of attention and feeling as a result of which an object becomes a subject: a *thing*.

It is the difference between merely glancing at something and really looking at it and entering into it. What happens? We are no longer indifferent, separate, 'detached' as I said last chapter, we open. And we open in such a way that is fundamental to feeling and being alive at all.

Mystics have always known this: that the world is not composed of inanimate matter — it is merely our lack of presence that makes it seem so. And poets have, too, and the only real difference between them is that a poet uses words. We choose to speak of these things. We want to communicate them.

Wordsworth knew this, and in his poem 'Tintern Abbey' (see suggested reading) in the lines beginning '... and I have felt/A presence that disturbs me with the joy/Of elevated thoughts...' he goes on to evoke 'A motion and spirit, that impels/All thinking things, all objects of all thought, /And rolls through all things'.

(Note the use of the verb he chooses there: rolls, with its slow mysterious grandeur).

Closer to the gound, Keats knew it too; he speaks in one of his letters about the experience he had of seeing a sparrow in the dust and of empathizing with it in such a way that he became it. No longer aware of himself standing separate or superior, all his heart goes out to a sparrow in the dust. It was a moment we remember him by, a moment which infused his writing... a moment in which, apparently losing himself, he found himself his real self.

Hopkins (an extraordinary innovator for his time, in the 1870s) knew this too. He knew poetry as a fusion between inspiration and science, a science you can hear in a line like 'Kingfishers catch fire, dragonflies draw flame', and he was often to be seen eccentrically, (so people inevitably thought), gazing at things in close-up... gazing and dreaming. Not dreaming as we usually think of dreaming, but dreaming awake, both waiting and wrestling for that particular phrase that would do justice to what he had seen again and felt again as if for the first time, 'now'.

We all have things: things we need, and things we don't apparently need.

You've no doubt had the experience of picking up something without particularly knowing why; you may even be surprised at the number of things you've gathered over a period of time. Things in poems are often of this second, subsidiary or 'useless' class. What is it that draws us to them?

What is it that draws a child to a snail shell? Or still, when walking along a beach, to find your eyes naturally combing among the pebbles?

Useless things (unlike, for instance, cars or computers) have this quality: that we can dream with them. The child in us knows this, as well as the dreamer.

Something inside us is drawn to something outside us, and in that meeting, often so casual, a door in us opens, and we see as we don't usually see; and the thing glows, lit up in its lustre.

It may seem immediately significant or synchronistic, or its significance may escape us for some time, for years even.

These are things of memory and things of the dream, as well as things of the present. Presence here expands our understanding and experience of time. It brings it to a different level.

We are looking at something and time stops. We are looking into it, entering into it with our eyes, as the moment expands, and the thing this flower, this rose fills it, and strangely fills us.

Gaston Bachelard, a French philosopher who abandoned orthodox science and its approaches, spent his latter years in the study of phenomenology ('the science of things'); and it is interesting that his study took him into poetry poetry and dreaming, or what he specifically called 'reverie'.

For Bachelard, things like houses, furniture and natural objects could neither be understood materially or psychologically. Bachelard resisted analysis either way. What he gestures is essentially poetic: a dreaming with, a making with. He leads with the intuitive right brain, rather than the analytic left brain. As a result, the world appears rather differently, it is a world closer to one we once knew, and at moments, continue to know: a world we each uniquely live in, dream in, dwell in; a world that, for him, becomes naturally round, whole, graced with wholeness.

Bachelard's preoccupation was 'the thing itself' or what he refers to as the image as opposed to the metaphor. He doesn't want language to *replace* the thing, he wants it to *reflect* it, as faithfully as possible. A language of things is visible and concrete. It is not abstract. It is a language of sensuality and touch. It is a language of earth.

Francis Ponge (who was a contemporary of Bachelard in southern France in the 1940s and 50s) practised this approach radically, so much so he was hesitant and at times uninterested in even calling himself a poet. For Ponge, this meant taking language back to the beginning. As he says: 'It is a question of a relation to the accusative' (by which he means 'you', or the world of objects become things). 'It is a question of the gravest relation not at all of having, but of being'.

Ponge set himself this task, and his poems or texts, often part--way in prose, record experiences of walking through a pine forest, or pebbles on a beach. As he says, 'it will make me become really aware and find joy afterwards'. His belief was that a poet should never offer an idea but a thing, he went as far as to devote the equivalent of short book on a single subject: a bar of soap!

Pablo Neruda, the Chilean poet who died in 1973, emphasizes this in what he lists as 'The holy canons of madrigal, the mandates of touch, smell, taste, sight, hearing, the passion for justice, sexual desire, the sea sounding...' (notice his inclusion of all the senses as well as the rhythm of his sentence). He goes on to counsel: 'Those who shun the 'bad taste' of things will fall flat on the ice'. Why will they fall? because, Neruda implies, they will not be really here.

Words, like things, have a life of their own. We're reminded of this when we hear a new word for the first time (I was, when I first heard the word tat, for 'stuff' or personal possessions). We tend to 'forget' words, as we become so used to them. And there is a way in which speaking quickly or tonelessly constantly blurs the sense and texture of what we are saying: we ride roughshod over it, or mouth it, or merely pay lip service to the language we use; we think we use language, and more often it simply uses us. It's always a useful exercise to pause over certain words; to hear the difference in weight and substance between, say, stone, wood, and flesh... and in this pausing, this depth, we are moving again from speaking into writing. Try it, briefly. Or as Basil Bunting wrote it: 'Pens are too light/Take a chisel to write'. Stone, wood, flesh.

Exercise: Finding the Thing

I'd like now to suggest this exercise to you, which is a little different from the previous three months, and which seems appropriate at this stage in the course.

I'd like you to reflect for a moment on the things you have in your room where you are reading this, just lightly, being aware as you look around of where they have come from and of how they have entered your life. Take a few minutes to do this, including the whole of your space. Don't hurry. If you are not in your own room but somewhere else, you may reflect on how the things that are there came to be there.

See, as you look, what effect these things have on you. Some you may pass over quickly, others you may look at for longer.

Be aware of the experience of what it feels like to look at these different things in each 'looking'.

Then, when you have completed looking round the room you are sitting in, choose one of the things you have looked at the thing which seems most to have held your attention. Your intuition will already know which one to choose.

When you have made your choice, go and bring the thing close to you, or if it is too cumbersome to move, move yourself closer to it.

Look at it. Make contact with it. Allow yourself to be with it.

Relax into being with it, rather than 'thinking about it'. Be aware of looking at and touching it, and of receiving from it.

Then take a piece of paper or your notebook and make a few notes. Allow what comes from it and you in your being with it.

Then, when you've completed your impressions for now, put your pen down and sit quietly with yourself for a moment. Close your eyes for a moment. Let yourself be still.

Now I'd like you to go outside. Leave your writing things behind. Go as lightly as you can, being aware of the stillness in you as you walk whether it is among trees or among traffic and people.

You are going out to find something, and you are going to let something find you.

You don't know what it is. How does that feel?

Will it be by the roadside? Will it fall out of someone's bag in front of you?

Will it be in a field? Or will it be in the sky?

Something is waiting for you. Keep walking.

It won't be what you expect. Keep walking.

It may be half an hour, or right outside your door.

And you will know when you find it. Remember, it may come at any moment.

It may simply be a glance or a gesture. So be attentive. There it is.

Then when you've found it, stand with or sit or kneel with it right where it is. Be totally with it.

Then bring it back with you, either in image or in concrete form (if you can).

When you're back inside, make some more notes (you might also want to draw it).

You now have two things: one from the past, the other from just now.

Taking whichever you'd like to work on first, I'd like to suggest you write from both of them. They may even be connected. And the connection is you.

See if you can allow what wants to come to come. Don't feel bound by trying or force what you want to write into a 'poem', or what you mentally might consider to be one. It may come as a poem or it may come as prose or poetic prose, as groups of separated prose lines or sentences.

See if in both cases you can let the thing, and your experience of it, speak. If you are having difficulty, simply go back to the thing. It knows what it is. You may find you make, or want to make, several drafts. You could even attempt several consecutive drafts on the same or different days as variations. It can be often like peeling the skin off an onion: each skin reveals something closer to the centre that the skin itself also reflects.

Study Poems

As well as writing, I'd like to invite you to really reflect on the study poems this time, making your own notes as you do. I've chosen three which seem to me directly appropriate: the first is by American poet Archibald MacLeish (the title of which reflects a Classical or 'classic' theme which is always in the process of redefinition across time). The second is by our previous Poet Laureate Ted Hughes, published in 1979, and the third by a contemporary who deserves to be much better known Paul Matthews (published in 1984) who teaches at Emerson College in Forest Row in Sussex. The sources for these are in the references and suggested reading as usual if you want to get hold of them. See what you feel about the poems, and see if you can note how you feel they work in terms of their phrasing and syntax. Be aware of the use of words in them, the movement of the words and lines they form, and the punctuation too. Reflect also on the 'voices' in them. Enjoy your time, may it be creative for you. In this 'red time' of the year (the season as I write this), this time of stubble fires and ploughing before seeding... which as Seamus Heaney reminded me is what a *verse* means: it means a line the plough makes, and as it turns.

ARS POETICA

by Archibald MacLeish

A poem should be palpable and mute
As a globed fruit

Dumb
As old medallions to the thumb

Silent as the sleeveworn stone
Of casement ledges where the moss has grown —

A poem should be wordless
As the flight of birds

A poem should be motionless in time
As the moon climbs

Leaving, as the moon releases
Twig by twig the night-entangled trees,

Leaving, as the moon behind the winter leaves,
Memory by memory the mind —

A poem should be motionless in time
as the moon climbs

A poem should be equal to:
Not true

For all the history of grief
An empty doorway and a maple leaf

For love
The leaning grasses and two lights above the sea —

A poem should not mean
But be

COMING DOWN THROUGH SOMERSET

By Ted Hughes

I flash-glimpsed in the headlights — the high moment
Of driving through England — a killed badger

Sprawled with helpless legs. Yet again
Manoeuvred laneends, retracked, waited
Out of decency for headlights to die,
Lifted by one warm hindleg in the world-night
A slain badger. August dustheat. Beautiful,
Beautiful, warm, secret beast. Bedded him
Passenger, bleeding from the nose. Brought him close
Into my life. Now he lies on the beam
Torn from a great building. Beam waiting two years
To be built into new building. Summer coat
Not worth skinning off him. His skeleton — for the future.
Fangs, handsome concealed. Flies, drumming,
Bejewel his transit. Heatwave ushers him hourly
Towards his underworlds. A grim day of flies
And sunbathing. Get rid of the badger.
A night of shrunk rivers, glowing pastures,
Seatrout shouldering up through trickles. Then the sun again
Waking like a torn-out eye. How strangely
He stays on into the dawn — how quiet
The dark bear-claws, the long frost-tipped guard hairs!
Get rid of that badger today.
And already the flies.
More passionate, bringing their friends. I don't want
To buy and waste him. Or skin him (it is too late).
Or hack off his head and boil it
To liberate his masterpiece skull. I want him
To stay as he is. Sooty gloss-throated,
With his perfect face. Paws so tired.
Power-body relegated. I want him
To stop time. His strength staying, bulky,
Blocking time. His rankness, his bristling wildness,
His thrillingly painted face.
A badger on my moment of life.
Not years ago, like the others, but now.

I stand
Watching his stillness, like an iron nail
Driven, flush to the head,
Into a yew post. Something
Has to stay.

THINGS

by Paul Matthews

What I'll miss most when I'm dead is
things that the light shines on.
If there aren't wet leaves in Heaven
then almost I don't want to go there.
If there isn't the possibility
of silly particulars
like library cards on a table
then I almost don't want to go there.
Library cards — because here some happen to be.
I am a small Englishman in an Infinite Universe
looking at library cards. That's funny.
In fact it frightens me.

I am in my room, surrounded by the things
which have somehow clung to my existence:
a picture of squirrels, a desk with inkstains
(it was my grandfather's before me),
a Buddha and a jar of Nivea,
a pottery lion lying among rosepetals.
These are my things. They comfort
and encumber me.

But Buddha, what about you?

Your sides are so sheer.
You gave all your riches away.
And can you still hold
on to yourself as a person?
Did Christ give you his things too?
He had a seamless garment.
The other things came when he needed them,
a coin in a fishes' mouth, ointment for his feet,
a crown of thorns.
Well, he didn't despise things.
He ate bread readily.
He loved the boats of his disciples.

*

And it's not just things that we love,
but one thing next to another —
this African violet beside the tuning fork,
this pen in my hand
as the rain outside falls among Quinces.
These things have happened before;
but when I happen to be there
and notice the shape of the space between them
then a new thing arises in the Universe.
This was unplanned.
This event without Karma.

Angels, though infinitely greater than us,
know nothing of this.
But Christ knows it.
He came for that purpose —
to write on a particular ground
with his little finger.

*

The Gods have enough of Immortality
and need things.
They need cuckoos in a damson tree,
they need rhubarb flapping beside a gate.
Their paternoster is an honest man
who can hammer a nail straight.

Suggested reading

Wordsworth, Hopkins; and Bachelard for a more in depth study.

Especially Wordsworth's *'Tintern Abbey'* (available most editions of his poems).

Kim Taplin *Tongues In Trees* (Green Books, 1989) see references.

Ann Morrow Lindbergh *Gift From The Sea* (Chatto & Windus). This brief novel, which has been frequently reprinted, is a classic of its kind.

Paul Matthews *The Fabulous Names Of Things* and *The Ground that Love Seeks*, available from him c/o Emerson College, Forest Row, E. Sussex (01342 822238) @ £10 inclusive of postage.

CHAPTER 5

INNER AND OUTER

'The purpose of a work of art is to stitch together the inner and the outer...'

— Robert Bly

INNER AND OUTER

A poem is a bringing of the inside and the outside in: a 'bringing' and a 'bridging'. This is true both in terms of experiencing a poem, and writing it (or allowing it to be written). Inner needs outer, and outer needs inner they are not merely terms in an equation.

So let's look at this 'stitching together': what it is, and what it implies.

Novalis (which was the pen name of the German Romantic poet, Friedrich von Hardenburg) wrote: 'The seat of the soul is where the inner world and the outer world meet. Where they overlap, it is in every point of the overlap'.

What he is saying is this: that our essential being, our centre, our creative being is not just something that is inside us, but it is something that comes into being, that happens, where we meet the outer. We are not autonomous beings. We are part of Creation. The illusion is that we are separate, and it is an illusion we pay a great price for.

We can see how inner and outer meet in our everyday experience. It is something that is happening all the time. Our experiences mirror this to the detail. We say, for instance, that we 'feel like the weather'. Or we can see, in a certain set of circumstances how what happens, happens from us as well as to us. We see our effect on events.

We can see the mystery of what happens at every turn; sometimes in moments that can take years to understand. We can learn to remember, and to read the signs. And we can see how we resist our experiences as well.

In any heightened experience, as Bly points out, there is an exchange of energy. Our energy goes out to something (a face, a hill, a sunset) and we receive energy from it. There is an exchange, which is the essence of the experience and is the essence of what we feel and remember. This is an energy that is physical, but also subtle. It happens every time we make love. There is a fusing-with, and a self-forgetting. We shift awareness, and become more receptive. We open.

Peter Redgrove describes how he wrote his first poem, back in the 1950s, 'After making love, a silence came into my head and into that silence came my first poem, complete. I was so surprised I nearly fell out of bed. I did get out of bed to write it down. I now realize that happening was a call to vocation: I realized what was occuring was a coming together of bodily happenings and mental happenings in a way I had never known before. In the act of love with a woman, it was not ordinary time, it was somehow out of usual time. Time stilled in me and to what had happened made an answer or response which was rhythmical speech, made up of images, a poem. I was astonished, it was like a voice, I think it was probably another personality inside me, the real Peter...'

It's a wonderful description. And it points to something we now need to look at: that as a result of two things coming together, a third thing is created.

The number three has ancient, associative connections, linked both to creation and to seeing.

In Hinduism and Buddhism there is the 'third eye'; in Christianity, the Holy Trinity, and among the pre-Christian Druids, the original creative Word was symbolized by three down-curving lines.

Out of two things, a third is created. We can understand this also as the apex of the triangle, which takes place as a result of the two points at the base. The point is that this third thing goes beyond the two things out of which it has come: it has its own existence.

Another parallel here is in philosophy. 'Thesis' and 'antithesis' are superseeded by 'synthesis'.

It's a leap.

The third thing here, of course, is the poem. It is what takes place in the 'overlap' as Novalis (who was trained as an engineer), says so precisely.

And it is a mystery. No one, mercifully, has ever been able to explain creativity.

What we can say, though, and what we can begin to under-stand as a result of becoming aware of this energy exchange in our experience, is that we are basically creative and that all our experience is latent, it is potential. So we begin to value our experience in a new way, as something ongoing, as this course itself is.

Poems synthesize our experience; a poem takes place between us and our experience. And it does something new: it takes us beyond both, into its threshold. The poet is in the poem and the experience is in the poem and the poem is distinct; we say 'it leads its own life'.

And this is why openness is so important. Poems surprise us if we let them! They have a habit of coming unexpectedly. You might like to pause for a moment and think of some of the poems you have already read here in this light, and the quality of surprise in them which is so much a part of their energy, and the way they work.

As Redgrove says so rightly, they take place in their own order of time, which is why they have often been referred to as 'gifts' and why writing poetry itself is a gift. However much a poem is subsequently worked on, crafted, reshaped, 'revised', its funda-mental sound and texture remains, and needs to, in its completion.

This is what inspiration means. Inspiration is an inbreath in which we suddenly find ourselves having to go inside. A stray line or phrase (from apparently out of nowhere, or from somewhere we partly already know), sets an unmistakable tone in which we know there's more to come... and already we are hunting for a scrap of paper, that pencil, that notebook. We're in the flow — we're alive awake and vulnerable. We have woken up.

What are we writing? What are we saying? Poems surprise us, not only in their coming, but in their content as well. A poem can be like a rare, unexpected child. Or classically (as with Mary Shelley's 'creation' Frankenstein), it can seem like something that is almost too much for us.

We guide a poem as we write it, and poems have a will of their own. Or rather, the energy in the poem has a will of its own, and a knowing of its own. Poets have often said that they don't fully understand what they have written and this can be a cliché, but as often it can be true.

It points to how much more we know about our personalities than we do our souls: and how the undercurrent of who we are, who we really are, is always with us, from the start.

Poems are personal in their origin, but as we write, the personality becomes transparent.

The personality becomes a vehicle for what is deeper and more enduring: for what it serves: and for what changes it. We will be looking at this more closely a little later.

Every poem is a discovery; a discovery and birth sometimes in spite of ourselves. Light and dark, light and shadow are both present here; and we may not always like what we find.

Put colloquially, poems can be sweet and they can give us a hard time.

We don't know, as we begin: we don't know, even as the first lines come to be written, and this is where the issue of self-censorship is so relevant. We cramp the flow, and we drop the stitches.

The stitching is in the moment, and the stitching is in the energy. It is first and foremost in our letting the words come (even as we are aware of shaping them as we do).

As the saying goes, 'the mind is a wonderful servant, but a lousy master'. So before I suggest some further writing for you to do, I want to add a few things about the creative process itself.

Poets have all had something to say about the creative process.

Keats described poetry as 'Soulmaking', Shelley evoked the poem in writing as a 'fading coal'; and in *Letters To a Young Poet*, Rilke counsels patience, not only in relationship to writing itself, but to its fulfillment in ordinary time, where, as he says, 'ten years is nothing'.

The process is enigmatic, and individual for each of us. It is as individual as we are, on our journeys in life; and it reflects those journeys. Some people write quickly, others more slowly: some poems come at one go, others, strangely, take draft after draft, because we know it still doesn't sound quite right, or feel quite right, or that something is still missing. The material for a poem isn't always entirely available when we begin it. Or it may be, in a flash.

The single, simplest and most important thing in writing is to be able to say yes to what is coming through. Poems require this of us, and unconditionally. And it helps when we realize what we are saying yes to: as difficult as that might also seem (not only in words, but in feeling).

Some people say poems are already written, all we have to do is write them down.

That can be so; but the working, the labour, the stitching of a poem is something that comes detail by detail from the moment of writing itself; the moment in which the words flow from us and beyond us. We are holding the space for them, and we are letting them go.

So what can seem like unstitching becomes the actual stitching. The unstitching is of our mental interference the stitching is the flow itself, our faithfulness to it, and our honesty in relationship to it. Honesty here isn't something legalistic it is to the feeling, and the words we feel that best reflect it, evoke it, and name it.

Every poem is a new challenge, or a new kind of acceptance; and the more often we can practise (even in taking down notes), the more used to and prepared for we can be when the moment comes. We create the moment, too, through our willingness we draw it to us. And again, that may take time: or human time, as we know it.

'Trust the process'. It isn't something neat and tidy, as clear as our intention and our desire may be. Poems are not isolated events. They build secretly... like bulbs under the earth. And there is a generosity about poems, too: there is always a second, third or fourth chance... if we give them a chance.

Inner and outer meet, like a marriage. And it's the relationship that counts.

Exercise: Connecting with Experience

So I'd like to suggest for this month that you choose an experience: which I neither wish to evoke or to circumscribe. It may be one you remember, or it may be one that is current.

What I'd like to suggest you do is that you connect to where you are and how you are feeling (particularly if the choice seems difficult) and to see what comes, or re-emerges in response to that. You may already have something in mind, and as a result of reading this.

What I'd suggest then, is that you attune or reattune to its energy, and let its energy fill you to the point where words start to spill, or come. The more you attune to the energy, the easier the words will come. And remember, in writing from your experience, to keep returning to its energy.

It's a wordless, feeling/seeing energy from which the words come, and it gives them and you the energy. So keep going back to the source; and if you lose the thread, be aware of what you need to get back to, or 'into'.

I'd also like to invite you to comment on it, not critically but in terms of where your poem or your poetic writing has come from.

Reflect on the process, about what it was like. Be aware of the details.

The process can be as important as the poem. We learn a little more, each time.

Concentrate on your own writing for this period.

Study Poems:

I've included three study poems which I think by now are self-explanatory in this context.

I've included them as pointers and as catalysts, and because they all embody this stitching, and speak to its implications... that reality which we strangely already know, and which comes as close to us as our own hands and eyes.

'All you need to do to write is to trust the void'.

Enjoy this time.

References and suggested reading follow.

SOMETIMES

by Hermann Hesse, translated by Robert Bly

Sometimes, when a bird cries out,
Or the wind sweeps through a tree,
Or a dog howls in a far off farm,
I hold still and listen a long time.

My soul turns and goes back to the place
Where, a thousand forgotten years ago,
The bird and the blowing wind
Were like me, and were my brothers.

My soul turns into a tree,
And an animal, and a cloud bank.

Then changed and odd it comes home
And asks me questions. What should I reply?

MYSTIC

by Sylvia Plath

The air is a mill of hooks —
Questions without answer,
Glittering and drunk as flies
Whose kiss stings unbearably
In the fetid wombs of black air under pines in summer.

I remember
The dead smell of sun on wood cabins,
The stiffness of sails, the long salt winding sheets.
Once one has seen God, what is the remedy?
Once one has been seized up

Without a part left over,
Not a toe, not a finger, and used,
Used utterly, in the sun's conflagrations, the stains
That lengthen from ancient cathedrals
What is the remedy?
The pill of the Communion tablet,
The walking beside still water? Memory?
Or picking up the bright pieces
Of Christ in the faces of rodents,
The tame flower-nibblers, the ones

Whose hopes are so low they are comfortable —
The humpback in his small, washed cottage
Under the spokes of the clematis.

Is there no great love, only tenderness?
Does the sea
Remember the walker upon it?
Meaning leaks from the molecules.
The chimneys of the city breathe, the window sweats,
The children leap in their cots.
The sun blooms, it is a geranium.

The heart has not stopped.

A THIRD BODY

By Robert Bly

A man and a woman sit near each other, and they do not long
at this moment to be older, or younger, nor born
in any other nation, or time, or place.
They are content to be where they are, talking or not talking.
Their breaths together feed someone whom we do not know.
The man sees the way his fingers move;
he sees her hand close around a book she hands to him.
They obey a third body that they share in common.
They have made a promise to love that body.
Age may come, parting may come, death will come.
A man and a woman sit near each other;
as they breathe they feed someone we do not know.
someone we know of, whom we have never seen.

Suggested reading
Novalis *Hymns To The Night*, translated by David Gascoyne and
Jeremy Reed (Enitharmon Press, Hants)
    Robert Bly's timeless anthology *News Of The Universe - poems of
twofold consciousness* (Sierra Club Books, USA & Green Books,

UK).

Rilke's *Letters To A Young Poet*, translated by M.D. Herter Norton. These letters, written to Franz Kappus between 1903 and 1908 repay several readings.

Transformation, ed. by Jay Ramsay (CHRYSALIS). Send a cheque for £8 to the address in Further Information on p153.

Into the Further Reaches – an anthology of Contemporary British Poetry celebrating the spiritual journey ed. Jay Ramsay (PSAvalon, 2007)

CHAPTER 6

THE JOURNEY

We shall not cease from exploration
And the end of all our exploring
Will be to arrive where we started
And know the place for the first time.

— T.S.Eliot

THE JOURNEY

Poems follow one another. Poems follow one another just as a sentence, that is apparently finished, contains the seeds of another sentence that follows it. Poems lead to one another in this way, and often in ways that we are not fully aware of at the time.

The connections can be subtle, not only in terms of theme (what we are writing about) but also in terms of the words we use and find, and the echoes between them.

We begin to see that there is something continuous at work here, which not only occupies the space of the poem, but which moves in the spaces between poems.

There is a thread, however tenuous... however often it is apparently broken less in reality perhaps, than by forgetfulness, inattentiveness, and all the other things of life which call on us.

Meanwhile, the process is continuous; and the thread is the journey.

'You are the path', as someone once reminded me. And what they meant by that was that 'you' and the 'path' are the same thing something we can all too easily divide by thinking there is somewhere we should be going; somewhere pre-planned and pre-ordained.

Or put it another way: I am not the tarmac on the road I am walking down, but I am where the road is going. And I both know and don't know where it is going — it wouldn't be a journey if I did.

Inner and outer, known and unknown: and as ever, it is both. And this is what a journey is: we don't altogether know where we are going, and we don't altogether know *who* is going.

The journey is the space where we discover these two things coming together. It may be a city we are walking towards, and it may also be a mirror. It is both. And it is in this sense that we can understand the other, inner meaning of the word journey as pilgrimage. An airport and a runway may be part of it, but this isn't a tourist outing.

We are travellers in time.

Pilgrimage is a heart word. It means our hearts are in it. And in a certain sense, too, it means that while we can choose to go, we've also got to go.

The journey draws us. We feel a pull to go, just as we do simply to leave a room. And it's not so simple and maybe, ultimately, it is very simple. I don't know yet.

The journey motif is fundamental in literature, and it echoes some of what we've already begun to explore. The classic journey and legend in our own culture here in Britain is the Grail quest, and the story of Arthur, his knights and the women, recorded here and in France in the 12th Century, and dating from six centuries before in history.

It retains its appeal and now more than ever, in terms of its 'Waste Land', it retains its relevance. It speaks to our hearts. It is a story, and it is more than a story it is a quest, a quest for the heart that the Grail symbolizes, and a quest also for the renewal of the kingdom. It is a quest studded with adventure and mystery, with unexpected happenings and unforeseen resolutions, exemplified in Gawain's meeting with the Green Knight, and Parsifal's with the Star Woman.

What separates the knights from the Grail Castle is their process and their journey, a journey at once of realization (self-awareness) and initiation (self-change). Inner and outer are constantly interwoven in the dream... and these days we could as well say that the Grail is the Earth.

It is the same with John Bunyan's *Pilgrim's Progress*, first published in 1678. Christian journeys to truth, and the truth of himself, leaving the *City Of Destruction* and passing through phases that are as feeling as they are real and real for all of us: the *Slough Of Despond*, the *House Beautiful*, the *Valleys of Humiliation* and *Of The Shadow of Death*, and the tract that separates vision from the reality of vision: the *Celestial City*, that became Blake's *Jerusalem* and Blake's *Hymn*.

We could say he journeys through parts of himself in the characters he meets, parts the task of his journey is to integrate and superseed.

The same could be said for Shelley's *Alastor* (which I've quoted from as one of the study poems), who lived and died and sung in solitude in so far as it also symbolized a part of Shelley that was out of relationship with people around him. Alastor journeys into the void and into surrender; and he stands for what is alone in us, and dies alone into a truth beyond images a journey that Eliot echoed in his own *'Journey Of The Magi'* .

The mystics call it 'the razor's edge'; and as D.H. Lawrence said in his contrary and inimitably honest way, 'it is better to journey than it is to arrive'. I think he also meant that we can so easily lose sight of the journey itself by focussing on the end or goal of it; and that's equally true.

'D'Oú Venons Nous? Que Sommes Nous? Oú Allons Nous?' (Where have we come from, who are we, and where are we going?), as Carribean poet A.L. Hendriks puts it in his contemporary poem of that title.

To ask a question is to open up a space, and as we know, it's sometimes more important to hold a question that it is to answer it. Poetry brings us to the depth of our journeys and the height, and the breadth too. Writing opens a door, and who is it who passes through that door?

We are an amalgam of memories, thoughts, facts and imaginings; certainties and suggestions; ends and beginnings. We are creatures of the dream and of awakening. And there is more.

There is what holds it strangely all together, that makes it flow through, that continues it, that 'is living our lives at the same time as we are living it' (as I once found myself writing).

We all have a sense of who this person or being is, and the more we journey, the more we come up against different aspects of it, and all it is related and connected to. It is a journey that takes place on different levels, like interconnecting layers of colour, between our dreams and our waking, our doing and being, and our sleeping. Some of it is familiar and some of it is not. Who have we been all our lives? How real have we been to ourselves? What's really been happening? I don't think we can avoid these questions. To begin to address this is what it means to come into the chrysalis; this inner space not just of our imaginings, but actually of our whole being.

We are like our own journeys, and journeys (as John Moat once remarked to me) 'are entities'. We can see this on any journey we make, particularly at a time of increased significance, where what is inside us and outside us become part of one dynamic stream, just as a poem does.

And there's a sense in which we're always walking in a poem, written on the living air around us, with all its countless nuances and signs that gather and pause and pass away like parts of a silent, lucid piece of music, alternately tremulous and soft, rapid and still, visible and like the misty rain in this valley through the squares of my small, high window invisible, the ridge with its trees blurred; the sky come down over it.

This moment of writing... and it's not just this moment, but what has come to it and what goes from it. The more we become sensitive to this, the more we deepen our awareness of time and our memories and origins, the more our awareness becomes attuned to each moment, and each subsequent moment, so that the moment itself is no longer isolated, no longer a freak chance, a wild meaningless sweep, but always part of something larger that surrounds it and infuses it with presence, and our presence.

It builds; it gains substance, just as poems do when they come grouped together over a period of time. The poems themselves gather these moments, these memories and their distillation; and as we see through, them we see, increasingly, with our own vision. Our way of seeing things.

It may be a new vision, but it is also somehow the way we've always seen things, so we are also reminded. We are reminding ourselves. There is something we are remembering, like something on the tip of our tongues, but calmer, more knowing, more knowing and less forced, for all the effort we also need to make.

It's like climbing a mountain (to quote an age-old metaphor) before the sky opens up at the summit, and we look down, and back on the way we have been, and forward to the edge of the spreading clear or cloud-rimmed horizon, into the sun.

It is something we do inside ourselves whenever we write, or prepare to write. We journey to writing just as we have journeyed to what we are writing. It is a raising of awareness and of the requisite energy. It is a climbing up and, equally, it can be a going down.

The energy required is the same, as Dante knew in a dark wood, meeting his guide Virgil 'in the middle of my life's way'. For Dante, it was a crisis: a crisis and an opportunity. He had to find the thread. He had to take the step, and being 'lost' was what brought him to it.

I think we all know that one...

Where we have come from is where we are going to: the depth of our origin is the depth of our return.

For many people, writing is a reconnecting with something that has been lost, or covered up, or fearfully suppressed. Fearfully, because it can be frightening to live our truth, and the only end of fear is in the truth itself. The end that is the beginning is each beginning. And actually, the only beginning.

We can see this looking back over our lives at different parts of the journey we have made, different as it is for each of us;

sometimes as a clear progression, at other times, as a transit of broken lines; and then again, more like a series of stepping stones. Different parts are scored in different ways. And it can change. The more we make sense of it, the more it finally flows.

Exercise: The Journey of Your Life

So, I'd like to suggest an exercise for you and this time you will need drawing paper and some coloured pencils or crayons.

Sit down with them comfortably in front of you, on a table, or a working surface; then close your eyes. When you're ready, breathe gently and slowly quieten yourself and your mind down.

Start to focus, as you do so, on the idea of 'The Journey Of Your Life', attuning to the overall sense of it so far, letting your awareness go back through it, and back to you to where you are sitting. Try simply to feel it, and feel the energy of it at different times, without dwelling long on any of it; but moving back, then moving forward as freely as you can.

Then when you're ready, open your eyes and make a drawing of it, using whatever colours feel right for various stages, and really see if you can let your intuition and your drawing hand guide you, allowing whatever shapes, images or symbols to come up in your imagining as you do.

Some parts of the journey may be vague, some clear, others jagged and others smooth; again, really see if you can include all these things allowing each of them to take their place in the whole as it emerges on the paper in front of you.

You may surprise yourself, seeing what you are doing... and remember: this is not meant to be a perfect drawing, it's for you to relax and let it come.

Go with the energy while it's there. It may take minutes or much longer.

Then when you've completed it as far as you need to, rest with it looking at your journey so far.

What I'd then like to suggest is that you see what comes from it. You may want to take notes, or write from it (seeing things you weren't aware of before) in a notebook or journal; you may want to write it up fully in prose from the drawing... or what may want to come is a poem, or even a group of poems over this coming time.

Don't worry if nothing comes to start with. The experience of the drawing may be sufficient to itself, or to start with. It may be a seed for a whole process. These drawings can be powerful and can last for some time, rather as early maps lasted drawn by their cartographers.

We all have our own map, of course. Our life map. It helps to make it visible. See what it begins to release in you, not only as a drawing, but as a gathering of energy both in it, and between you and it. Stay with it. Live with your drawing each day, rather as you would with a painting you've chosen for a wall. I'd advise you to live with it yourself. And sometimes talking about it can help, at an appropriate moment. Be your own judge here. It's your life, remember!

Study Poems

The study poems I've chosen are all on the journey, and I've arranged them (as before) so that they make a kind of journey in themselves in sequence. They point to some of the different levels we've touched on here; and they are all in their own way meditations on direction, choice and memory deep memory, in the case of the Frances Horovitz poem, which echoes past life material that some of you may share.

Go well, as they say. As we say, before a journey.

from ALASTOR

by Percy Bysshe Shelley

The poet wandering on, through Arabie
And Persia, and the wild Carmanian waste,
And o'er the aerial mountains which pour down
Indus and Oxus from their icy caves,
In joy and exultation held his way;
Till in the vale of Cashmire, far within
Its loneliest dell, where odorous plants entwine
Beneath the hollow rocks a natural bower,
Beside a sparkling rivulet he stretched
His languid limbs. A vision on his sleep
There came, a dream of hopes that never yet
Had flushed his cheek. He dreamed a veiled maid
Sate near him, talking in low solemn tones.
Her voice was like the voice of his own soul
Heard in the calm of thought; its music long,
Like woven sounds of streams and breezes, held
His inmost sense suspended in its web
Of many-coloured wool and shifting hues.
Knowledge and truth and virtue were her theme,
And lofty hopes of divine liberty,
Thoughts the most dear to him, and poesy,
Herself a poet. Soon the solemn mood
Of her pure mind kindled through all her frame
A permeating fire: wild numbers then
She raised, with voice stifled in tremulous sobs
Subdued by its own pathos: her fair hands
Were bare alone, sweeping from some strange harp
Strange synphony, and in their branching veins
The eloquent blood told an ineffable tale.
The beating of her heart was heard to fill

The pauses of her music, and her breath
Tumultuously accorded with those fits
Of intermitted song. Sudden she rose,
As if her heart impatiently endured
Its bursting burthen: at the sound he turned,
And saw by the warm light of their own life
Her glowing limbs beneath the sinuous veil
Of woven wind, her outspread arms now bare,
Her dark locks floating in the breath of night,
Her beamy bending eyes, her parted lips
Outstretched, and pale, and quivering eagerly.
His strong heart sunk and sickened with excess
Of love. He reared his shuddering limbs and quelled
His gasping breath, and spread his arms to meet
Her panting bosom:... she drew back a while,
Then, yielding to the irresistible joy,
With frantic gesture and short breathless cry
Folded his frame in her dissolving arms.
Now blackness veiled his dizzy eyes, and night
Involved and swallowed up the vision; sleep,
Like a dark flood suspended in its course,
Rolled back its impulse on his vacant brain.

from THE FLOWERING OF THE ROD

by H.D.

II

I go where I love and where I am loved,
into the snow;

I go to the things I love
with no thought of duty or pity;

I go where I belong, inexorably,
as the rain that has lain long

in the furrow; I have given
or would have given

life to the grain;
but if it will not grow or ripen

with the rain of beauty,
the rain will return to the cloud;

the harvester sharpens his steel on the stone;
but this is not our field,

We have not sown this;
pitiless, pitiless, let us leave

The-place-of-a-skull
to those who have fashioned it.

XI

He was the first that flew
(the heavenly pointer)

but not content to leave
the scattered flock,

He journeys back and forth
between the poles of heaven and earth forever;

He was the first to wing
from that sad Tree,

but having flown, the Tree of Life
bears rose from thorn

and fragrant vine,
from barren wood;

He was the first to say,
not to the chosen few,

his faithful friends,
the wise and good.

but to an outcast and a vagabond,
today shalt thou be with me in Paradise.

from HELLO

by Robert Creeley

River wandering down
below in the widening green
fields between the hills
and the sea and the town.

Time settled, or waiting,
or about to be. People,
the old couple, the two babies,
beside me the so-called

aeroplane. Now
be born,
be born.

JOURNEY

by Frances Horovitz

now is the time for walking in woods
by the cold stream come from the waterfall
are you afraid?
    no but the path shifts
here I am safe
    but the path shifts under my feet
I walk on but the leaves are black
    and grab at my face
I remember the carriage
    craning impossibly
        by the side of the waterfall
there was no shifting —
    the firm boards
        held us together
            over the waterfall

but all that is past

I saw the long steel slip into the groin of the roof
their feet clumsy but quiet on the ancient eaves
I screamed I knocked into furniture
like a bat I blundered in terror —
    they ran down the stairs
        like chimneys of blood
    they caught the young men
        in the dark cellars
    the places of slaughter
        the animal sounds under the knife
    the kitchen midden
        the black dank on the wall

all long ago —
there was a sharp instrument
     a musical bow
I touched
     it gave off a sound
disturbing the dust

they were hanged in the open air
   wrapped in their grave cloths a woman among them her face
crumpled she swung as the mask moved like the half of a nut it
slipped from her face
   it fell
the crowd breathed sharply
   was still
horror   the mask fell
   her face was the same

in her same face she will walk again
   in the woods
   in the house of her choice
I will meet her again in the shifting woods

Suggested Reading

Robert A. Johnson's *He*, which tells the story of Parsifal and Emma
Jung / Marie Louise von Frantz's classic *The Grail Legend*, a must
for in-depth appreciation.

Bunyan's *Pilgrim's Progress* (at least a glance at it), Eliot's
'Journey Of The Magi', and the beginning of Danté's *Inferno*. Danté
meets Virgil in a dark wood at the beginning of *The Divine
Comedy*.

H.D. and Frances Horovitz are recommended. Creeley's
poems are interesting in terms of 'writing on the move' and 'in the
moment'. *Hello: A Journal* is a medley of short or 'minimalist'
poems written on a journey he made through South East Asia.

D.H. Lawrence's *Selected Essays* (Penguin), especially the pieces about travel in Italy, Germany, Mexico and New Mexico.

Somerset Maugham's short classic novel *The Razor's Edge* (Pan), is the story of a mystic cally Larry, which I found memorable.

Journey to Eden by Jenny Davis and Jay Ramsay: available from 5, Old Farm Lane, Sidmouth, Devon EX10 9TX for £7.50 including P&P (Cheques to Jenny and Glyn Lewis).

CHAPTER 7

THE JOURNEY OF POETS

'By a knight of ghosts and shadows
I summoned am to tourney
Ten leagues beyond
The world's wide end
Me thinks it is no journey...'

— Tom O'Bedlam, Anon (quoted by Kenneth Patchen in his *Journal of Albion Moonlight*)

THE JOURNEY OF POETS

And so we come to the journey of poets. What does it mean to journey through poetry?

What, in the end does it mean to be a poet? If life is a journey, then poetry is a journey twice over or more than twice, perhaps many more times than twice as it is a journey both in experience and in language.

It is a choice and a compulsion, a burden and a liberation, a labour and a letting go.

It is a suffering of meaning to give birth to meaning. It is a gift given to be given.

It is a journey to the essence, as we see it: and a journey for the sake of that alone.

Poetry is an intensification of life, for this purpose: and poets, with all their individual differences, share this. It is a particular intensity of mind and being that is basic, and which we all have in us. Poetry both requires this, and evokes it as we recognize.

We can feel the energy, and our own in response to it.

Plato, in his *Phaedrus*, called this the *daimon* of creative inspiration, it has been recognized from the beginning. He was talking about what makes a person into a poet, what happens to her or him, and pointing to something enduring: which is that in a very real sense there are two of us. There is the person and there is the poet in the person: there is an outer skin and an inner dreaming body; and there is the tension, the dynamic, between the two that that creates. It may begin as an idea, and it becomes a way of life, as it has to in order to be expressed and embodied.

In any poet's life, both are present. And if we look at the lives of poets we can see that it is not an easy relationship, particularly as a result of the Renaissance which gave rise to an emphasis on individual consciousness, something which we now take for granted.

Plato had long since exiled poets from his State, and had predicted at long range the journey that was to come. Instinctively, he know poets didn't 'belong', and perhaps he knew their task couldn't be fulfilled if they did.

For the bards who came later, poetry was an initiation that required not only mastery of memory, but a mastery of being in which both creative and destructive energies were understood (symbolized in the Celtic 'Cauldron Of Ceridwen' the seething material of the world).

For poets closer to us in time, without the protection of the tribe and the collective, the experience has been very different. As I pointed out in the Introduction, it has been one of separation, a separation in which wholeness itself has been split and one in which recognition of the value of poetry has diminished. As the centre of things has been increasingly dominated by material consciousness, so poets have gone to the periphery: to the edge.

But if poetry has diminished, the energies involved in it have not: and this has been reflected and mirrored in poets themselves: in their lives and in their work, and in the relationship between the two. The dilemma broadly has been one of relationship to creativity and inspiration, containment of it (emotionally and psychically), and embodiment: both personally and materially. Response to it has been unique, and forged even in the face of death: the pain has been one of disjuncture, between inner and outer, self and world, and this is a common thread.

'How can a man live who has been the Glory?' cried Christopher Smart in his *Jubilate Agno* (see references). And Wordsworth, in his poem about meeting the leech-gatherer on the lonely moor, reflected: 'We poets in our youth begin in gladness/But thereof in the end comes despondency and madness'.

Wordsworth suffered the decline of inspiration, and his own need for solidity brought him finally to work as Laureate and as a financial inspector. Rimbaud, beside Blake, the most searingly honest of poets, gave up poetry altogether, to return to the earth, as he saw it, and become a man. Walt Whitman, the American, whose voice rings through the film Dead Poets Society ('carpe diem', sieze the day), never gave up, and espoused an open-hearted democracy that had him reading his poems to station coach drivers on Broadway. Rilke pursued a single-minded quest for purity through solitude, which took him finally to Muzot, where, after ten years of blockage and frustration, he completed his *Duino Elegies* in an outpouring of days.

Yeats struggled to bridge his private and his public life, drawn between inner work, writing, and action in the Ireland of his time: both in theatre and as a Senator, without compromise.

Less than twenty years later (in 1953) Dylan Thomas was dying in a New York hospital of chronic alcohol poisoning. Jack Kerouac, who used benzedrine and dope, followed him, and ten years after Dylan Thomas, Sylvia Plath was found lying in her kitchen with the gas oven open. Harry Fainlight, Thomas Blackburn... there have been others, too.

There are extremes here, and I'm quoting well-known poets as examples.

In a world where 'values' (in inverted commas) have been orientated towards economy and warfare, poetry as a counter-force is an extreme gesture. Its very extremity shows how far we have come away from the reality it represents. And there is another side to this, because we are all human.

There is the light of the quest, and there is the shadow of personality or ego, which poets are by no means exempt from. In fact, these aspects can be magnified because of the energies involved as they were with Dylan Thomas, who for all his fineness, as a poet, became a victim to the Dionysiac quality he was working with: and Caitlin, his wife, suffered accordingly.

Among poets generally, alongside sensitivity, there is a tendency towards evasion and dependency that runs like a parallel thread. This is a complex issue.

The crisis of being thin-skinned is very real and it cuts both ways. Creativity is shadowed by destructiveness, self-destructiveness where the work and the life fail to meet. You can imagine this as two halves of a circle. Where all the energy is put into the poetry, the life – the living of it – invariably suffers.

It is an imbalance that becomes narcissistic and at its worst becomes a rejection of life by art. The result may be genius, but it is impotent. The very energy it seeks to release becomes trapped. It becomes a distortion, and the purpose can get lost.

Susan Hill's portrait of the fictional poet Francis Croft, in *The Bird Of Night*, is relevant here (see references). Madness, in this sense, is the outcome of an energy that is neither fully contained or embodied, as opposed to being a process of healing and purification. It is a fine balance.

Confucius has a saying (quoted by Ezra Pound): 'It is easy to go to extremes: it is hard to stand firm in the middle'. At the same time, the pressure to survive can reinforce these very things, with tragic consequences.

A late worksheet of Dylan Thomas' has draft lines and phrases interspersed with a list of debts; and poetry, despite changes, still remains a largely unpaid commitment.

What we can say, then, is that poetry requires a greater and not a lesser discipline, not only in terms of its fruition, but because of what we go through as poets in expressing it.

So what is this process, and what does it entail?

Poets each have their own way, that corresponds to their inner being; and there are common characteristics that are echoed in biography, for example a solitary childhood, or an experience of being singled out by circumstance that in retrospect can seem (as it did for me) like a kind of preparation.

Life shifts towards the inner, and what is outside is taken within. We call it 'dreaminess' for some years, perhaps, before words first come. It is an unconscious process, that pre-dates being a poet, or being called one: but things gleam as they are seen, felt and remembered, and an aptitude for precise seeing and remembering that is so much part of being a poet is seeded. 'Poeta nascitur non fit' (poets are born not made) in the old Latin phrase; and my feeling is that it is both, because it is a process.

As Jeremy Reed puts it, recalling his earliest memory of a bullfinch his mother pointed out to him: 'I have gone on adding to that picture, magnifying the bird until it has become a symbol of poetry itself'.

Poets each come to poetry individually: for some it is a gradual experience, for others more abrupt. You will remember my quoting Peter Redgrove in 'Inner and Outer' on this.

And you may like to pause and think of your own. We come to it, and it comes to us... suddenly, the snow, as if dreamt, flaking down outside, whitening on the uncut grass and the sloping field.

Something of this freshness is in a poet's earliest poems; in essence, they echo a beginning, just as last poems resonate ending. Poets grow into their voices, and you can often see a shedding of past influences as that emerges: the quest is for authenticity, for what rings true, and the poem is a constant exercising of this. This is its particular tension, and what holds it in shape, in form. Every poet has a distinct tone, within which some poets have a greater range than others.

For Yeats, development meant a deliberate changing of style to accommodate what he had to say, and as a reflection of his journey from the 1880s to the 1930s (he died in 1939).

A poem journeys to itself, either in one writing, or through a series of drafts, and we'll be looking at this in more detail soon. Writing itself is both sedentary and active: it comes out of an inner stillness of being that allows the movement of a poem to take place. There are variations here.

Wordsworth used to pace a gravel path composing in his head, and he would frequently walk his poems, like Shelley (in

Italy) who often wrote outside. Yeats, up in his tower, would hum and sound out the rhythm of what he was writing, or about to write.

Ezra Pound, who did so much to introduce new form, wrote, like e.e.cummings, straight onto a typewriter to judge the length, flow and break of lines; and Kenneth Patchen (their contemporary) wrote the whole of the *Journal Of Albion Moonlight*, lying on an injured back, on large sheets of drawing paper that were then transcribed.

For most contemporary poets the activity is interior for practical reasons (either at home, or for some, on retreat). Every poet has their own way of rooting or anchoring, and that is important to find in a turning, floating world.

I have said that the journey motif is fundamental and this is true for poets in differing degrees, and on different levels. For some, like Pound, it is overt, and his modern epic *The Cantos* is a vast 'sailing after knowledge', unfinished at the time of his death in 1970, in which he threads the mythic metaphorical figure of Odysseus through a shifting pattern of what he called 'luminous details', weaving history and politics together with reference to different cultures and languages, including Chinese ideograms.

On a more personal mystical level, there is the Greek poet George Seferis who specifically titled sections of his work as 'log books': making his quest through the transparency of the imagination itself, and through seeing things that way. On the other hand, with Philip Larkin, and his more existential and provincial concerns, there is little sense of movement beyond his first collection *The North Ship* (1945); and for other poets, the journey is more discrete and, perhaps, assumed.

Invariably, poets see things in different ways, and with different responses, but they all leave footsteps, and every poet's work is essentially autobiography in this sense.

Poets are part of place and time, and they are also more than that, and some are more conscious and deliberate in this respect than others. For each, being true to the path and the calling describes a different shape that brings the poet and the poetry together, just as in the poetry, inner and outer and brought together.

Every journey is like a different angle on the centre, and we can see how each poet does a different work that at the same time is part of the whole, a whole that includes and goes beyond the sum of its parts. I think we need to learn to see poetry more in this way.

All poets share, as we all do, essentially a senstitivity that connects them indelibly to their inner being, and to the collective (the world).

The journey of poets is a quest for meaning, particularly in this century. We call it 'coming to terms with', and it is that, and it is more than that.

A poet has something to say, and suffers the saying. A poet has both an ego, and an 'I' that goes beyond it, and 'I' deeply connected with his or her vision, and the process of its incarnation.

As Alan Jackson says: 'This story... is all I'. This process is indistinguishable from an inner passage which has to do with, as I once put it 'living up to our depth'. It is a shedding of skins, a shedding of everything that finally separates us from who we are.

Rilke saw this, and lived it: for him both Creation and the Divine was in a process of evolution: and evolution of consciousness and its realization.

Poetry, more than any other art, seeks to communicate this, through language, and through keeping language alive. Consciousness here is a consciousness of language, as well of what moves behind, within, and through it.

A poem is a signal to the world; and poems have varying degrees of intensity in this respect. And because poetry is a feeling art, every feeling has been and is relevant.

Creation itself is distilled in poetry through feeling, and all its different shades, from gold to ashgrey, from rage to tenderness, from passion to serenity.

This is what poetry takes on, and poets do likewise: and this is what their names and their work represents.

A poem is a gesture: and imagination is the bridge, both to our inner selves and from them, to the world. Our world.

So why journey? Why bother? For what? For a poet, it may be death to do so, but it is certain death not to. It is a risk this risk of flight, and landing. And it is life we are looking for, at the root and among the ruins. It is witness and proof, and the way there.

Meister Eckhart, the 14th Century radical German theologian, has a four-fold path, comprising of *positiva, negativa, creativa,* and finally what he calls the *via transformativa*: the way of compassion and social justice.

Poetry, by its very nature, has always been preoccupied with values both from a religious and secular point of view. As Blake said, 'everything that lives is holy'.

Poetry and poets have, as a result been inevitably in opposition, both silently, strategically and vociferously. You can see this like a lifeline running through every tradition: in Blake, Patchen, Russia, and among the women and men writing in Britain now.

Shelley, in exile, called poets 'the unacknowledged legislators', and that legislation remains to come into being. Poetry is naturally political in this sense: it is the consequence of sensitivity. And politics and spirituality must come togeher, as we are now beginning to realize, beyond the ethos of negativity that has infused late nineteenth and twentieth century writing.

Where poetry meets the world, it meets embodiment, and its need to be embodied. It is standing for what we believe, it is standing in our truth, or as the Native American Indians say, 'walking your talk'. This is where poetry speaks from the heart: it is what is personally felt that we all feel, as we know when we talk with one another. It is what is felt and made present by being present, by communication. And for poets increasingly now (including myself) this is what it means to share and perform the work as a vital part of it.

To hear a poem read or performed well is a spur. It is a release of energy we are looking for; a release of what has been held for so long in words on paper. This is why I have suggested you also read the poems aloud. You can feel the life being breathed into them and you can feel it in yourself. It is one and the same.

At the same time, the inner journey remains as a necessary complement: because we cannot change anything unless we change ourselves (and we do far more by opening ourselves than we know). Alan Jackson prefaces his *Heart Of The Sun* with an extended introduction called *'Reasons For The Work'*, and for many poets now, many outside the literary mainstream, poetry is 'work' both psychologically and spiritually. This is the journey.

There is a growing awareness now of what poetry is, and is for what it serves and a growing sense that it is not just 'I' either, it is we. This is a personal appendage. Where, in the end, is the journey to? Where else but to what is right here in front of us, the Eden we have lost and are returning to: the world's back garden we all live in.

The purpose of poetry, in the end, is this freedom: to make, as Ezra Pound said, a 'paradiso terrestre' (heaven on earth), to help make what the planet itself is destined to become, that is insepa-rable from our own fulfilment and realization: to see and realize, as Dante saw it, the 'love that moves the sun and all the other stars'.

And the way through to it, to that? Well, it is happening.

It is happening now.

Exercise: Your Journey as a Poet

What I'd like to suggest you do for this month is two things. The first is to evaluate your journey as a poet, tracing the thread of it through your life's journey that you've been reflecting on.

See if you can get an image for this thread, and where it has led you, or tried to lead you: when it has been visible, and when it has disappeared... the way dreams do, underground.

And again, follow it up to this point in your life. You may have written poetry before as a child, or at school for a time; or you may never have written anything until now: or you may still be waiting to write – it doesn't matter, the thread will be there if you allow yourself to be still and reflect on it. I would like to suggest you imagine this thread, and having done so, ask it what it needs from you now. You may get a word, or another image, in reply. And it may point you to a particular part of your being or your body as well.

The second thing, which is optional, is for you to choose a particular poet you like as a result of what you have read or been reading and study their life in this respect. It may be a poet you feel naturally drawn to by empathy or identification, and that can be very useful.

I'd like to suggest you write from this, as well as from the exercise above: either in poetic or prose form. See what comes.

You may also want to reflect on the study poems on this theme, and what they are saying.

What do you feel about them?

We will be moving on to more practical things relating to you and your writing in the next chapter.

References and suggested reading follow, as before.

Study Poems

RIMBAUD

by W.H. Auden

The nights, the railway-arches, the bad sky,

His horrible companions did not know it;
But in that child; the rhetorician's lie
Burst like a pipe: the cold had made a poet.

Drinks bought him by his weak and lyric friend
His five wits systematically deranged,
To all accustomed nonsense put an end;
Till he from lyre and weakness was estranged.

Verse was a special illness of the ear;
Integrity was not enough; that seemed
The hell of childhood: he must try again.

Now, galloping through Africa, he dreamed
Of a new self, a son, an engineer,
His truth acceptable to lying men.

EPODE

by David Gascoyne

Then
The great Face turned away in silence, veiled and slow,
Resigned and imperturbable: the brow
A grave dome drastic in its upthrust, and the eyes'
Unquenched blue fires of grief sealed and concealed
Beneath lids of irrevocable flint. It turned
Away; and as the shaft below began to slant
Towards its headlong fall into unknown
Futurity, the sacred Mouth enshrined
Like a sarcophagus within its midst revealed
During that moment's timeless flash
The wordless Meaning of the Whole

(Which may be spoken by no man)
Through the unearthly brilliance of its smile...

While the old world's last bonfires turned to ash.

(from ORTS)
POETS

by Ted Hughes

Crowd the horizons, poised, wings
Lifted in elation, vast
Armadas of illusion
Waiting for a puff.

Or they dawn, singing birds all
Mating calls
Battle bluff
And crazy feathers.

Or disappear
Into the grassblade atom – one flare
Annihilating the world
To the big eyed, simple light that fled

When the first word lumped out of the flint.

INCARNATION

by Gabriel Bradford Millar (née Lanny Kennish)

Allow for the fact that

The soul is a cheetah,
> flashing and swift,
> that finds life

Difficult in captivity:
It hears across the land
> the running of flanks
> on familiar dust

By the fierce mouthside
The long black strands
> are melancholy.
> Not that it should

Avoid the condition,
Refusing to fix
> in the mindblasting,
> miraculous chamber

Where spirit meets grit
> For the first time,
> like tumbled stone.

PILGRIM WOMAN

by Pippa Little

This is my map: a square of crumpled cloth,
the continents scratched with my fingernail.
Though far, far out between two worlds
I know where I'm going.

This interim of yellow, fetid dark, clenched

hands, the sweated pain of travelling
this must be done with soon.

Don't comfort me
don't make me weak.
I need endurance now
to focus
my one deep eye, a red jet burning.
For this I concede confinement, torture.
If I lose resolve
I'll fall to the sea floor, die again
and again, breathe only sour water.

In answer I dream of my landfall,
my horizon-curved ledges
stone warm to the warm skin of my hands and my feet:
a whole, brownskinned and straightbacked land,
rivers of good, strong blood in me
singing from sun to moon.
Here my lost, uncharted years
hang, lambent fruit, deep
in blue trees of the interior.

I wake to want,
again, to wrench this caul, this blindness
from my head, rise up and use
these wasting bones. Already I
have carved my footprints on the shore.
I want to press my feet deep inside those prints!
I want to shed
my old selves quietly,
emerge
emerald and shining,
jagged as a dragonfly.

Don't touch me:
don't hold me back.
Instead
I step from my body's ship
on to the salty stones.
Safe,
delivered,
triumphant,
everything is before me.

Suggested reading

From the above (from what draws you): I would suggest Kenneth Patchen *The Journal of Albion Moonlight,* Susan Hill's novel *The Bird of Night,* Jeremy Reed's *Madness, the price of Poetry,* Alan Jackson *Salutations,* Arthur Rimbaud, David Gascoyne, also Gabriel Bradford Millar (nee Lanny Kennish) in *Transformation* (ed. Jay Ramsay) – see references.

For Eckhart see Matthew Fox's *Meditations with Meister Eckhart.*

For contemporary poets in the last 25 years, see *Angels Of Fire - an anthology of radical poetry in the '80's,* edited by the present author; as well as *Into the Further Reaches – an anthology of Contemporary British Poetry celebrating the spiritual journey* (ed. Jay Ramsay). See p. 131.

Biographies: from a good library or bookshop, where you can enquire and see what they have on screen if not immediately in stock. Many smaller bookshops have this facility now as well, so you can order through them.

One outstanding example is Enid Starkie's biography of Rimbaud.

CHAPTER 8

MAKING THE SPACE

'But, you may say, we asked you to speak about women and fiction; what has that got to do with a room of one's own? I will try to explain.'

— Virginia Woolf

MAKING THE SPACE

For all of us, writing means making the space; to translate the idea of it into actuality. Our need for space is basic to both our needs and our psyche. It is as necessary in waking as sleep is for dreaming. We all sleep and dream: but how many of us have the space we need?

In a very real sense, when we write, we expand. We occupy more space than we do in ordinary consciousness. And this space is fragile. It can all too easily be broken. Coleridge's legendary 'man from Porlock' (that interrupted his writing 'Kubla Khan') is a metaphor for all of us, not only external, but internal. We all have a man from Porlock in us. We distract ourselves, too.

Virginia Woolf recognized this, with acuteness, subtlety and humour. Asked to give two lectures on the subject of women and fiction, she found herself (as *A Room Of One's Own* narrates) talking about everything that separates one from the other. A few years later, her contemporary Cyril Connolly made a similar inquiry from a male point of view in his *The Enemies Of Promise* (1935). Like Woolf, he was pinpointing aspects of negative social conditioning, like the public schools of his time. Both books are dated, and both are relevant. We may have changed our clothes and our slang; things at the root take longer.

There is a tension, inevitably, between the circumstances of ordinary life and artistic work; and the whole art becomes how to make this into something positive and creative which reflects us and which we can claim as ours. The tension, or the crisis, is the opportunity.

Artistic work tells us that life as it is, as we live it, is not enough. There has to be more. And without life as we live it, as we know it, we wouldn't know this. That is the dynamic.

It is one which I sense many of us are feeling now, in this time of change. So much we have been used to for better or worse is no longer working. Old patterns and structures are dissolving. Walls of every kind are coming down. We are being shown different priorities. Things are changing from the inside. We are being reorientated.

In all this, it is vital to find a centre: both outside us, or around us, and inside ourselves.

I always remember going to visit John Fairfax at his thatched cottage near Hermitage in Berkshire. He'd come to it through a thicket of brambles like the prince in the fairy tale. It had been near derelict for some time, and piece by piece, he'd had to work on it.

Standing there in the sunlight with him, near where he was chopping wood, with the grass shining behind him, it all seemed as it was so complete. We were talking about finding a new way to live. 'Yes,' he was saying 'and you have to create it'.

It begins inside us, as it did for John, writing his early work in London before the need to move came. It begins inside, and what is basic here is making a space in which we can write, or begin to write. Outside reflects inside here: the more we consciously create this space, the more we nurture, affirm and strengthen the space in ourselves. So it begins with a desk or a table in a room: it begins in a circle that is protected, and there is something ancient about this it is like the *temenos* of the old temples, the space in which initiation took place.

Modern therapy recreates this in the context of a session, but in this space we are taking about one of us. I am talking about you. The difference between poetry written in the corner of a room, and written where it can enjoy its own space, is reflected in the writing itself. For myself, over ten years now, I've become increasingly aware of this; increasingly aware of how the space I give myself effects the potential of what I'm doing: its pace, it rhythm, its height and depth; and for me this has been particularly true of longer or sustained pieces of work.

It is like weaving a cocoon that holds both the work and me; it is invisible, and yet palpable, and it takes place in one particular room, as it always has. I have to set boundaries in relationship to friends, the phone, the post coming through the door... and it's not perfect, and I still don't get it right. It's not perfection but it is an intention, an intention that builds up energy daily, even when nothing seems to be happening. It might go on like that for minutes or days, and then it continues. I get a 'strike', and the words flow again and it's all there. But it is just as important that I am there when it, apparently, is not. It isn't something that I can control; I can only make myself available, increasingly, to it. It takes skill and patience, not only the strong will of commitment, but the skilfull will of flexibility. It's like lovemaking in that sense: or as the psalmist said, waiting on the Lord.

So what are the strategies? There is home, as I've been saying (and I'll be coming back to that). The second thing is holidays, or free days, which can be naturally conducive and inspiring. We relax, withdrawing from the usual kinds of pressure which constrict us and the sense of routine and familiarity that dulls us is replaced by newness. Our inner energy rises to it: the contours of everything are sharper and brighter. We are somewhere else, which can help us be somewhere else in ourselves.

Lawrence Durrell (who was always drawn to Greece) gives an evocative picture of this in *Prospero's Cell*, his travel journal-/novella about Corfu, which he wrote as a young man before going to Alexandria. As he says: 'It is April and we have taken an old fisherman's house in the extreme north of the island Kalamai. Ten sea miles from the town, and some thirty kilometres by road, it offers all the charms of seclusion. A white house set like a dice on a rock already venerable with the scars of wind and water. The hill runs clear up into the sky behind it, so that the cypresses and olives overhang this room in which I sit and write. We are upon a bare promontory with its beautiful clean surface of metamorphic stone covered in olive and ilex: in the shape of a *mons pubis*. This is become our unregretted home. A world. Corcyra.' (Corcyra is the old name for Corfu).

Of course, things have changed since Durrell was there, as they have on all the other well-known Greek islands since the late 1970s, and this is true through most of Europe though remote places like the coast of old Yugoslavia north of Dubrovnik remain. So we need to choose where we are going, and some of the lesser known or less overtly commercial travel companies can be of help. Odd places can turn up, too. I remember arriving on the island of Elba, Italy, and after spending half the night driving round it, thinking we'd made a complete mistake, then coming to the unspoilt terraced slopes of Patresi Colle, with its primitive beach down through a spring wood. And there are places here, as I have found in North Wales, if we're willing to look for them: wild places where the space is open, and we can become one with what surrounds us, and listen. You can take the elements of your own creative space with you: not only your laptop or notebook, but a few things that are relevant for you to make your own space when you are there. It might not seem like much, but it can help us to dwell and to focus.

Another option is to go on retreat; many religious communities support themselves by offering this facility. Writing itself is always a retreat and retreats are ideal for inner work which requires us to be inside with what is already within us.

Retreats are complementary to taking holiday space, and their tone is different. It is an absence of external stimulation that can be just as effective, depending on who we are and where we find ourselves on our journey. And again being in an unfamiliar place, that is also 'safe' (protected) can help us to be objective, and to hold to our objective. Retreats have their own pattern; it usually takes a day to adapt and prepare, and the next two days can be difficult as we negotiate the inner space: the feeling, form and tone of what we are attempting. Usually, it deepens then, and we get into it.

Our awareness shifts, and because it isn't being pulled back, gathers resonance (you may feel lighter in your body if you go out walking). It gains momentum, and comes to its own height; before slowing, to end for the time being. Often, other things manifest: or as my friend Carole once said to me: 'See what's also trying to happen'.

On holiday and on retreat, the process is similar. We may not know what we want to write, or what we do write may be unexpected either way. We are receiving energy or evoking it, in faith; and we need to follow it, like a stream, to 'stay with it'.

It will establish its own rhythm of periods of concentration or immersion; and it may be one that is unfamiliar to you in terms of habitual clocktime. Time, as you know, passes fast when you write. Time itself becomes more spatial, and in the space that what we are doing occupies. Holding the space, and holding it lightly, is essential – not that it's always easy. But it can be like being a fine stylus poised above a hairline vinyl groove, and the temptation is to become inadvertently complacent. It can seem easy, too, almost ridiculously so. And then the drawback is to doubt it. My own learning here has been to stay with the energy while it is there, and go as far as I can with it before pausing. It's both an effort and a surrendering to the work as it takes molten, fluid shape...

There is a useful diagrammatic image here from modern psychology, of a circle surrounded by a box or square, at the centre of which is a point. The circle is the space, the square is its boundary or surrounding, and the point at the centre is the focus. The circle is feminine, the square masculine... and I was reminded again recently of the Egyptian hieroglyph for the sun, which is a dot at the centre of a circle. You might like to draw this for yourself and reflect on it. It is both an outer and an inner reality. Sometimes we need to develop the circle, or at others, the square. Or again, the focus at the centre, if we are scattered.

Writing is a grounding of energy in words, as well as a release or expression of energy through them, and we need to be practical about it; and to get to know our strengths and weaknesses in relationship to it.

It can only improve from there. So I want to look finally at this in terms of its implications for how we live.

Coming home is not an end, it is a beginning. It is a coming home to ourselves, and to a centre that holds. Home, heart, and hearth are all synonyms for this – you can hear their sound as they blend together – but above all, I am talking about a place in ourselves. I am talking about a centre and a circle.

Perhaps being homeless allows us to understand this more deeply: but how many of us are at home in ourselves? And how many of us are at home where we live? It may be a convenience, but in reality it is much more; and it is a reality many of us have lost touch with, we are neither at home in our homes, in ourselves, or on the earth; and these three things are one thing, one effect. As Othello says 'it is the cause, it is the cause, my soul'. And where else are we closer to tragedy now than on the earth itself?

Home has been clouded by sentimentality and commercialism. But what 'home' really means is to dwell: to be, to stay, to remain. And dwelling is something deeper than living as we know it.

Dwelling means receptivity. It means being wholly in touch with. And it is an indwelling, for me encapsulated in the soothing call of a wood pigeon.

Coming home to myself, I begin to live as I am. And at a certain stage, nothing less will do. There is a leaving and a finding here: we have to leave what is false or inappropriate to find what is true. And this is an inner process as well.

We do it where we live, and we could be living anywhere.

I had one friend (the healer Ted Partridge) who lived in a converted tram on the seafront at West Wittering, Sussex, and he chose to be there to do the remarkable work he did.

Poets have known this: the power of being at home, even in poverty.

Milton knew it, so did Blake, so did Wordsworth. The way they lived was voluntary; they knew that only by living that way could they have the discipline and rhythm necessary to do what they were doing. The American poet William Carlos Williams came to find his major work, *Paterson*, was based at home. Bachelard, whom I have already mentioned, talks about this in terms of what he calls 'intimate immensity'.

So to practicalities: what becomes obvious is that we each need to find and create our own rhythm that gives a home to our gift, and is reflected by it – and there is the key. The more individual we become, both in ourselves and in relationship, the more we need to live it, and live from it. And it is there the work begins. How are we going to live our days? When we are going to write, to shop, to pay bills, to meditate? How can we earn the money to do it? What is a luxury, and what is necessary?

What do we need to do as well as to write? What else is our creativity asking of us? This is the workshop floor, or if you like, the bare boards under the carpet.

Exercise: coming home to ourselves

So I'd like to suggest an exercise for you to do in this context, and again it will be useful if you have some paper or notebook to hand.

Sitting comfortably, just be aware of your breathing; of the air coming in and going out, and then the rise and fall of your abdomen. This is centering. Allow yourself a clear minute to do this: then close your eyes. Go inside to the centre of your being, and be aware of it as you come to it, and what it feels like to be there.

Then, taking a moment, begin to connect to the feeling of the gift you have, however embryonic it might be or seem. See if you can feel it rather than think it. It will be the first feeling you have. It may surprise you. You may also see an image of it, or for it. Be open either way.

Then, holding the space in your awareness, see if you can ask this feeling or image, 'What do I need to do to allow you into my life?' and 'How do I need to live to honour you?'

Two questions. Take them one at a time. You may receive a word or phrase, or another image in response. Either way, be aware of it. It will be important. Ask each question, then when you feel you have received the answers, see if there is a third thing you need to ask... and if not, see if there is anything else your gift wants to communicate to you.

Then, when you're ready, come back slowly and make some notes; including what feelings came up for you. Then, closing your eyes again for a moment, gently breathe down from your belly, down through your thighs, calves, ankles and feet into the earth... which is grounding.

What I'd like to suggest now is that you begin to think practically about what you need to do to live for your gift, and the gift that is you.

We are all gifted and in the deepest sense, what we are is 'given'. How have you been living in relationship to this? What do you need to do to change it? How clear about your needs have you been in this respect? With others, and with yourself? How does the space you live in reflect it?

Have you made room for it? Have you welcomed it?

There are some questions, which you may already have. See if you can look at your life and yourself through these questions in terms of now. There may be things from the past that need to be cleared, things that have waited for you to become conscious of them.

There is always a timing to realization of any kind. Rilke has a poem, 'Archaic Torso of Apollo', which ends suddenly with the line 'you must change your life', and I can still see the moment when that line flashed back across me.

We are in the chrysalis, dreaming of coloured wings and flight, of the sun, and the slow lengthening of the light.

No one ever told us we were allowed to dream our lives. So dream it now. This time for real. Let it come in pieces, as you build up this image of your creative life.

Then write what you can of it, in poetic or journal form. It may come as a poem or prose-poem in essence, or it may be an ongoing diary. Give yourself time to do this, and see what begins to happen for you as you do it. You may want to take space away to do this. See what you feel.

It is more, much more, than an exercise. It is you. Be well.

Study Poems

from THE PROPHET

by Kahlil Gibran

Then Almitra spoke again and said,
And what of Marriage, master?
    And he answered saying:
    You were born together, and together you
shall be forevermore.
    You shall be together when the white
wings of death scatter your days.
    Ay, you shall be together even in the
silent memory of God.
    But let there be spaces in your togetherness,
    And let the winds of the heavens dance
between you.

    Love one another, but make not a bond
of love:

Let it rather be a moving sea between
the shores of your souls.

Fill each other's cup but drink not from
one cup.

Give one another of your bread but eat
not from the same loaf.

Sing and dance together and be joyous,
but let each one of you be alone,

Even as the strings of a lute are alone
though they quiver with the same music.

Give your hearts, but not into each
other's keeping.

For only the hand of Life can contain
your hearts.

And stand together yet not too near
together:

For the pillars of the temple stand apart,

And the oak tree and the cypress grow
not in each other's shadow.

NOW SUMMER IS GONE

Arseniy Tarkovsky, translated by Kitty Hunter-Blair

Now summer is gone
And might never have been.
In the sunshine it's warm.
But there has to be more.

It all came to pass,
All fell into my hands
Like a five-petalled leaf,

But there has to be more.

Nothing evil was lost,
Nothing good was in vain,
All ablaze with clear light
But there has to be more.

Life gathered me up
Safe under its wing,
My luck always held,
But there has to be more.

Not a leaf was burnt up
Not a twig ever snapped...
Clean as a glass is the day,
But there has to be more.

AFTER THE DARKNESS

by Rosemary Palmeira

Life
pulsing through my veins
the relief of blood
running, rushing back
notes spilling from my fingers
echoing wildly
the thrill of finding harmony
welling from unpractised hands
yet a deeper knowledge
of earth and river
swells from its source
finds it channel

Waking from sleep
the solid sap in my skull
density of fallen cloud
softens, slowly melts.
Sudden, a gush of breath
clear and lucid
oh the gift!
the heart's shaping of life
clenched in my hands.

And so it was
that my strength returned
I stood up tall
and saw all things clearly;
the earth grew richer
the trees full and heavy
and golden flowers shook
in the sedge at evening.

Live coals in a grate
beat against the rib cage
this
slow rising yet
foundation sure.
I know things at their root
I shall not be dazzled by brightness
nor fall in a dark instant
my arms flexed in bronze
my body arched in light.

Suggested Reading

Kahlil Gibran's *The Prophet* is required reading, and widely available.

   A Room Of One's Own by Virginia Woolf, Lawrence Durrell,

and *In The Gold Of Flesh* edited by Rosemary Palmeira.

Rilke's poem *'The One Birds Plunge Through'* and Edwin Muir's poem *'Nothing There But Faith"*. (see p. 132).

Susan Hill's *The Magic Apple Tree*.

CHAPTER 9

THE BUTTERFLY

The emergence of a butterfly from the chrysalis is always a most interesting operation to observe, and everyone should make a point of watching the process, so that practical knowledge maybe obtained of how the thing is done.

— *The Observer's Book of Butterflies*

THE BUTTERFLY

I want to end this part of the course by drawing together some of the threads we've been exploring over these months in a creative meditation.

I keep seeing wings as I reflect on this: they are large, golden-yellow and translucent shimmering like sunlight, like light through thin curtains ruffled by a slight breeze. The window is open. Leaving the chrysalis takes us to a new level: it is the leap I have spoken of that every poem makes in the moment and moments of its coming into being.

In reality, every poem recapitulates this process: so we leave the chrysalis, and we return to it by returning, each time, to the source and the seed.

*

If the top of an egg is examined under a good lens, a depression will be noted, in the middle of which are minute apertures known as micropyles (little doors), and it is through these that the spermatozoa of the male find entry to the interior of the egg and fertilization is achieved.

We have seen how essential, and not only how essential, but how creative, vulnerability and openness are in poetry so that inner and outer can meet, as we do, in relationship.

We become porous as beings, and underneath our everyday armour, this porous quality is already there and is entirely natural, much more so that the accretions of our defensiveness and their shutting or blotting out of feeling and sensation.

We were made better than we make ourselves, and at a certain point, it becomes vital to become natural again, to become authentic... and particularly now, if the new days are to come.

We know this porousness, and it is through it that experience, our experience, enters us and seeds us. We know we are not as solid as we seem: we are lighter, more dynamic and vibrant; and we are growing despite everything, and because of it, towards the consequences of that.

We are going to become butterflies.

Experience enters us, slowly, or in a flash – and we can even come to know it is happening while it is happening: the moment is all around us, and in us as we stand inside it, and we know that 'This is important. I'm going to remember this'. We may or may not know why (at this stage) but we know nevertheless.

Something we are seeing or sensing becomes an idea, a possibility, a latency as yet without form, and as yet without words, or with only a few of them perhaps.

The bare impulse is what comes first, that is both specific, like a nerve or thread, and general: overall a mood or atmosphere that fills and encompasses the visible space of where we are, and in which everything is a part, everything is connected.

Everything speaks, in silence or sound, in whispering or birdsong, in through our ears and eyes and through the surface of our skin.

We are full of little doors... and we can see how already these openings and this openness prefigures emerging from the chrysalis.

The oak is contained in the acorn, and every stage of this linear process is also circular; circling round and moving forward through itself.

Already I am seeing the movement of a caterpillar...

*

The second stage is that of the caterpillar, and in some species this is of very short duration, a few weeks only, whilst in others, it usually lasts for many months.

The moment of seeding can be rapid: the process of incubation can take longer. It may be days or years. We don't work to a tidy schedule like an office; our psyches are richer and stranger than that, and the order that things come or unfold in can be a mystery: one, which in retrospect is usually connected with readiness.

As Shakespeare put it in *Hamlet*: 'Ripeness is all'.

I have thought that the time it takes to write a poem is in some way equivalent to its original inspiration: short poems can happen in a flash, and where the idea and the writing fuse like lightning. Longer poems may encompass weeks or gaps of weeks, where the original experience took an hour or hours, but we are at a different level of time here, and measurement in one sense is irrelevant. 'Only the Father knows the time'.

Gillian Allnutt, a contemporary poet and friend, expresses this suggestively in a last 'Notebook' entry in her poem/-journal/novella *Spitting the pips out*:

'It has been there for several years. I have started writing it at least three times. I have tried to force it to go on when it didn't want to. It is like a snail that sleeps its slow life away, dreaming its unknowable dream of inside the shell. It comes out occasionally to test the air with its unaccustomed antennae and leaves an almost invisible trail of silver words across the empty page. Then it goes in again. Then one day it comes out and there is my book.'

She sees it for what it is: a feminine, inchoate process she gives a particularly feminine allowance to, and by extension, this is true of the feminine in all of us, of what is, literally speaking, seeded in our soul and in our innermost being.

She also points to something important which has a direct analogy with the caterpillar's fasting and shedding of skins that take place: that the interiorization of an experience is an experience itself in and through which we become as fine, or as finely attuned, as what it is we have to say.

This is another way of looking at readiness and ripeness:

experiences, and the knowing or understanding contained in them, often come to us ahead of time, and there is a sense in which we are 'ahead' of ourselves as we go towards the future and the future flows towards us, drawing us by an inner magnetism.

So we can push away (this is part of the labour), but at the same time we need not to... and this goes against the grain of what we have been taught and how we have been encouraged, negatively, to be where 'being' isn't valued at all especially here in the West.

And (as with inner and outer) it is both in terms of our energy.

A plane taxis down the runway; and then the engines roar. And at the right moment the roaring is easy like light, like a river, like a cry that almost unbearably becomes a song.

*

Finally, however, when the caterpillar has shed its skin for the last time, the chrysalis is revealed, but with the future wings seemingly free.

This process is consolidated inside the chrysalis and its hardened shell. It is a shell, not armour: with the crucial difference that armour is something you can't easily, get out of. Like an aggressive 4-wheel drive, it becomes a habit.

The shell, on the other hand, is a voluntary and necessary protection that corresponds to what we were looking at in 'Making The Space'. It functions to minimize outer distraction and unwanted interference, and to maximize inner concentration and fermentation.

The chrysalis is a centring, a coming-to-centre in this sense. And in so far as it is also something we walk around in as well as our sacred space or room, it is a shield that allows us to retain the state of mind and being we are in, as in: 'I'm sorry, but I don't want to talk at the moment'. Or rather, 'I can't talk now. I'm already talking to myself'.

And it can be flexible as well. Another old friend, the actor Russell Denton, likened concentration to a slowly heating kettle, and when an interruption has finished, what do you do? You put it back on the boil. There are degrees of this. Often, we are having to do various things at any one time, or in one period of time, and to isolate these strands can be helpful.

Our chrysalis can have more than one dimension, where strands of work can be usefully isolated from one another, rather like wavelengths. That way, they can also nourish each other. We can come to one particular strand by way of the others, either directly, or with the energy we need and we have been lacking the confidence, even.

The other thing here is preparation, which also has to do with holding our intention or intent. You can stare and stare at a scrap of paper with notes for a poem on it and get nowhere until it starts to come, but the very action of doing that affirms and reaffirms it, even if you think, 'I'll never be able to do this'.

We grow into the moment this way the way a mountain grows into the sky: its sky.

Succinctly put:

In passing to the chrysalis stage, the caterpillars sometimes have to make rather more preparations than in previous skin-changing provisions.

You might like to pause for a moment and evaluate your own.

*

The moment of a poem is ineffable. Already it has come.

Already the wings... already the sense of passing into its accelerated, fluid awareness.

And we may feel in no way ready for it, and yet we are.

I'm thinking of Carole writing a poem on the back of a bag on a bus, crossing Putney Bridge: eight or ten lines, straight through, for her friend Marian, then gone recently to Ireland.

It isn't always like that; usually, it is harder work, altogether more like labour and more human. It comes in spurts, with pauses, and then it comes again. But whatever the difficulty may be, and it is always variable, the moment itself is essentially the same. It begins to speak...

*

When the butterfly is ready to emerge, the shell of the chrysalis splits along the thorax and at the lower end of the wingcases, and the insect is then able to release itself from the pupal trappings. The manner of the breaking open of the chrysalis shell varies in different species.

There is an opening, which corresponds to our initial openness: and while gradually we may get to know this and come to feel it is the one that is really our own, the almost numb sense of wonder remains, not as an exultation (though it may be that!) but as a necessary prerequisite for our being open enough to allow what wants to come to come.

The wings may be sky blue or black, yellow-green or dark blood red, and each is a different experience in feeling, pulsation and tone. Ash grey poems feel grey, like mist or rain. Some poems read like ice. I touched on this in 'The Journey Of Poets'.

My own experience is of heightened awareness, and heightened care: of an immeasurably rapid holding on, or holding on to, and letting go. I am aware of sound, image, meaning and shape simultaneously and I am learning about each, second by second.

Pre-knowledge can be a problem: but the stronger the impulse, the stronger the splitting, the more that knowledge comes with and as the energy itself. And then, curiously, I'm relaxed: even diffident, although by no means indifferent.

For me, to get a good draft from the moment itself is important. The more I have, the more choice I have. I don't mean by this a quantity of words, but a quality of thoroughness, of 'throughness' in relationship to what the poem is.

This first writing is the most vulnerable: it is literally what comes from inside the chrysalis. The butterfly is struggling to break free.

As Eliot put it in *Four Quartets*:

> 'Words strain,
> Crack and sometimes break, under the burden,
> Under the tension, slip, slide, perish,
> Decay with imprecision, will not stay in place,
> Will not stay still.'

He is pointing both to the moment of writing, and subsequent drafts where they are necessary.

Perhaps we can gain some wisdom from the butterfly here in terms of its emergence.

For when it breaks free, it doesn't simply fly. Something else happens first that is of primary importance.

Having safely cleared itself free of the chrysalis shell, the butterfly makes its way to some suitable twig from which it can hang, usually in an inverted position, whilst a very important function takes place. This is the distention and drying of the wings, which at first are very weak and somewhat baggy, although the colour and markings appear on them in miniature. All other parts of the butterfly seem fully formed, but the helpless condition of the wings alone prevent it as yet from flying off into the air.

In a very short time, after the insect has settled to the business, the fluids from the body commence to flow and circulate through the wings, and these are seen gradually expanding and filling out until they attain their proper size.

When the inflation is completed the wings are kept straight out for a time, they are then motionless, but all their surfaces are well apart. The wings being now fully developed, the further flow of fluid appears to be arrested.

This, for me, points to something deeper in terms of trusting and letting the poem be, not only as it first comes, but afterwards as it in a very real sense 'hangs', particularly if it seems unfinished, there, and yet not fully there (not yet).

The issue of making drafts is contentious.

T.S. Eliot laboured and crafted his *Four Quartets* (especially *'Little Gidding'*, the last one).

D.H. Lawrence, on the other hand, came to believe that drafts artificialized the original being and shape of a poem which he saw as another manifestation of control mentality, and he refused to work on many of his later poems.

Dylan Thomas, whose poems give the impression of such spontaneous ease, worked up to 48 drafts of single poems (like *'Fern Hill'*), constantly rewriting and crossing out, and making lists of potential words for insertion.

Two contemporary poets express the same issue, both in interviews. Carol Rumens says:

'Form is everything. It can be improvised or invented, or borrowed from tradition, but form there has to be'. The late Ken Smith, also a London poet, adds: 'The more drafts, the more chance of the poem getting lost in the paperwork'.

Both can be extremes, and both are true and we will be going on to look at all the implications and possibilities for form in the continuation of this course.

The real point here has to do with fidelity to the original impulse and spirit. The process of writing a poem is an incarnation, a clothing in a body of audible and readable words, and the whole point of working on a poem is so it can have wings: that it can live and move fully formed both on and off the page.

I thought to include three examples of my own here, from a poem called *'Grace'* I started at an isolated cottage by the sea near Porthmadog in North Wales, in April 1987. The poem went through three drafts before its completion, and I'll quote the first stanza of each so you can see how the opening changed. This was how it started, rather uncertainly:

> The sun a fiery white pearl, the cloud-sky
> Spreading its light over the estuary water,
> The still tide held between ebb and flow
> The silver grey water and mist-covered mountains
> The distant shoreline houses, the line of the cobb
> And the horizon the strong winging sound
> Coming in to splashland, and float slowly
> Up towards this rock;'

I am describing the landing of a swan, as I sat outside on a broad shelf of grey rock down in front of the cottage. I am trying to re-evoke the sun, the atmosphere of the sea mist, and the unforeseen moment of the swan's landing out of it; and though the gist is there in terms of description, the pacing isn't right... I feel it goes too fast... I'm missing some words... it's not quite expansive enough.

So I tried it again:

> The sun a fiery pearl in the massed soft
> Slow whiteness of cloud, sky spreading its light
> Over the estuary water: and the tide, still, held
> Between ebb and flow... the silver grey water
> The grey mist-covered mountains... the distant
> Shoreline houses... the line of the cobb
> And the open horizon the strong winging sound

Coming in to splashland... and float, silently
Up towards this rock:

Well, it was better: the description was more precise and tighter, and I'd begun to get a deepened sense of atmosphere in terms of the actual rhythm of the lines. But it still wasn't right. The words were there, I felt; I didn't want to add any more words, but the shape wasn't. It was too compact. It needed opening out, so that it could breathe.

This time, I took it slowly line for line, marking each length and pause with my ear as my eyes watched the words coming up on the typeface. I wanted the right punctuation, too, balancing commas with dotted lines, the dash and finally the colon as you can see in this final version:

The sun a fiery pearl in the massed soft slow
Whiteness of cloud, sky spreading its light
Over the estuary water:
And the tide still, held, between ebb and flow,
The silver grey water...
The grey mist-covered mountains...
The distant shoreline houses...
The line of the cobb, and the open horizon —
The stong winging sound coming in to splash-land
And float
        silently
           up towards this rock:

That was it, as far as I could see (in the eye of the butterfly). I was then able to go through the rest of the poem to the end, holding its pacing and rhythm in relationship to how it then continues unfolding as a result, ending as it does with two groups of stepped lines (where the lines 'drop' or 'hang'), and four short lines together which punctuate it, and its 'downflow'.

So, despite moving away from the original in one sense, with subsequent rewriting, I felt I'd closened to it in another, and been truer to it.

With each draft, though, my mind was with the original experience and the sketch I'd made on the back of a smallish white envelope I'd had in my anorak pocket. That was what I'd sketched and jotted down then and there, and it was vital that I had it as a touchstone. As soon as my eyes saw it, I remembered.

I could go back to the source of it, and come back forwards to each of the three subsequent points I reached. Then I found I was letting it go.

To return to the butterfly, then:

The beauty of a butterfly's wing is intimately connected with the form and colour of the scales with which they are covered, as with a kind of mosaic.

And, in terms of what I've just been describing about returning to its source:

Colour is chiefly due to pigment contained in the scale or adhering to the interior of its upper side. Pigments are stated to be derived, by various chemical processes, from the blood while the butterly is still in the chrysalis stage.

The beauty of that, I think, speaks for itself.

Exercise: Reprise and Revise

So what I'd like to suggest you do is to look at what you've written in this light, and particularly poems you feel are incomplete either in words or in feeling (or both). I'd like to suggest you gather up what you have done and seen, and understood, too, over this time of working with this book, tracing the passage you've made, perhaps in a page or two (or more) of prose description, as I think it would be helpful for you to know – and I would very much like to know as well, if you are working with me.

We might also explore the possibility of continuation.

References and suggested reading follow as before.

This time, I would like the study poems to be your own...

Suggested Reading

from the above: Lawrence, Eliot, and Gillian Allnutt (who has poems in *Transformation*, as cited. See also Penelope Shuttle's poem *'Chrysalis'*, in there).

Victor Gollancz's *A Year Of Grace* (Penguin 1950). This remarkable anthology is well worth tracking down through secondhand bookshops. It's a classic.

Matthew Fox's *Original Blessing*

Further Reading

A general reading list for this poetry course follows:

Essential reading

The New Penguin Book of English Verse edited by Paul Keegan (2001) – or a similiar collection that covers (and contextualizes) the different 'ages' of poetry.

The Rag & Bone Shop of the Heart editors Robert Bly, James Hillman and Michael Meade (HarperSanFrancisco, 1992).

American poetry, also European examples in context. Illuminating psychological commentary/mini-essays.

Transformation – the poetry of spiritual consciousness

edited by Jay Ramsay (Rivelin Grapheme Press, 1988). A collection of 63 contemporary UK poets with an introductory essay about poetry and spirituality. Available from Chrysalis, 5 Oxford Terrace, Uplands, Stroud Glos GL5 1TW @ £7.95. Some copies left.

Into the Further Reaches – Contemporary British Poetry celebrating the spiritual journey edited by Jay Ramsay (PSAvalon, Glastonbury, 2007). 64 poets, with a short introductory essay. Available online from www.psavalon.com @ £13.50 (01458 883864).

The Essential Rumi – Coleman Barks (Penguin, 1999).

Fresh American translations from the Persian of this 12th Century Sufi Master.

Hymns to the Night – Novalis, translated by David Gascoyne & Jeremy Reed (Enitharmon). Available from 40 Rushes Rd, Petersfield, Hants.

Letters To A Young Poet – Rainer Maria Rilke (New Directions, USA).

Letters to Franz Kappus, 1903-1908, that repay much re-reading.

The Complete Poems - Arthur Rimbaud (d.1894),

translated by Paul Schmidt (HarperColophon, USA, 1979). Young French *enfant terrible*, the most searingly honest of poets, in these excellent and memorable translations.

The Prophet – Kahlil Gibran (Penguin).

Timeless sacred text from this Lebanese Christian emigre who lived in New York in the 1920s and 1930s. One of the best selling poems of all time.

Collected Poems – Paul Celan (d. 1970), trans Michael Hamburger (Penguin).

Famously 'difficult', Celan was a Holocaust survivor and suicide. His integrity is on the edge of language itself.

Classics

Gerard Manley Hopkins Selected Poems (Penguin)
Emily Dickinson (USA) Selected Poems (Faber)
Thomas Hardy Selected Poems (Dent)
W.B. Yeats (d.1939) Collected Poems (Macmillan)
D.H. Lawrence Selected Poems (Dent, or Penguin)

20th Century poets

Dylan Thomas Collected Poems (Dent)

T.S. Eliot (d.1965) Collected Poems (Faber).

Ezra Pound (USA-d.1970) Selected Poems (Faber)

H.D. (Hilda Doolittle) Selected Poems

e.e.cummings (USA) selected poems 1923-1958 (Faber)

Sylvia Plath (d.1962)Collected Poems (Faber)

Ted Hughes (d.1998) Collected Poems (Faber)

Frances Horovitz (d.1983) Collected Poems (Bloodaxe, 1985)

Kathleen Raine (d. 2003) Collected Poems (Golgonooza Press/Counterpoint, USA, 2000)

Peter Redgrove (d. 2003) Collected Poems (Penguin, 1999 – and updated)

Robert Bly (USA): any of his many collections since the 1960s, translations of Kabir and Rumi, as well as Herman Hesse.

All above books mentioned are available from most bookshops unless otherwise stated. Many individual poets you can trace through anthology collections and from bookshops, and online via their own websites and online book outlets.

Wild Geese by Mary Oliver (USA) is a selection, (published by Bloodaxe, 2003).

Salutations (Collected Poems 1960-1989) by Alan Jackson (Polygon, 1990) contact alan45jax@beeb.net and www.thewindis-blowing.com

Love Poems – Brian Patten (George Allen & Unwin, 1982)

The Ground that Love Seeks by Paul Matthews (Five Seasons Press, 1996) contact Paulmfmatthews@aol.com – or c/o Emerson College, Forest Row, East Sussex RH18 5JX

The Saving Flame by Gabriel Bradford Millar (Five Seasons Press, 2002) available from The Studio, The Lindens, Lower St, Stroud, Glos GL5

Vale Royal, Universal, The Unihabitable City, Salvia Divinorum – Aidan Andrew Dun (Goldmark, Uppingham, Rutland: 1997,

2002, 2005) contact AidanAndrewDun@aol.com

Anthologies

Freedom to Breathe – *modern prose poetry from Baudelaire to Pinter* edited by Geoffrey Godbert (Stride, 2002). Wonderful examples of this neglected form.

Other – *British & Irish Poetry since 1970* editors Peter Quartermain & Ric Caddel (Wesleyan University press, USA, 1997).

Good introduction to experimental and post-modern work, some of the best of it.

Grandchildren of Albion editor Michael Horovitz (New Departures, 1995).

Pop/performance poets, some musicians.

Available from 11c Colville Terrace, Notting Hill, London W11 or michael.horovitz@btinternet.com

Vespers – *Contemporary American poems of religion & spirituality* editors Virgil Suarez and Ryan G. Van Cleave (University of Iowa Press, 2003). Illuminating, diverse, always engaging.

Generation Txt edited by Tom Chivers

The beat goes on. Six young UK poets (penned in the margins, London, 2007). info@pennedinthemargins.co.uk

Literary criticism (and language)

The Adventure of English – *the biography of a language* by Melvyn Bragg (Sceptre, 2003)

A journey through the words that have found us.

The Making of a Poem – *a Norton anthology of poetic forms*

editors Mark Strand and Eavan Boland (WW Norton, USA, 2000). A good place to start with more awareness of poetic forms and their origin. Some lovely examples.

The Truth of Poetry – *from Baudelaire to the 1960's* By Michael Hamburger (harcourt Brace, New York, 1969). A classic of 20th

Century comprehension.

Madness, the price of poetry by Jeremy Reed (Peter Owen, London, 1989). Detailed and jewelled studies, including G.M. Hopkins and Dan Gascoyne.

Tongues in Trees – Studies in Literature & Ecology by Kim Taplin (Green Books, 1989). Recalling tradition (Keats), and ahead of its time.

The Song of the Earth by Jonathan Bate (Picador, 2000). More recent ecological studies.

The Heart Aroused by David Whyte (Doubleday, USA, 1998). Redeeming the corporate soul of America through poetry... by this transplanted Irish Yorkshireman.

Suggested further reading

An Imaginary Life by David Malouf (Picador) Novel about Ovid's meeting with his guide, a wild boy.

Magic Casements by Sir George Trevelyan (Coventure, 1982): personal anthology with his own illuminating commentary.

Winter Pollen by Ted Hughes (essays: Faber, 1994) includes his tribute to Eliot.

Love Poems by Kenneth Patchen (New Directions, USA). Special and unusual 'free' poems from this 1940's jazz poet.

Collected Poems by Tomas Transtromer (Bloodaxe). The Swedish Laureate, also a psychologist for many years (d. 2003).

Gift From the Sea by Ann Morrow Lindbergh (Chatto & Windus). Classic prose-poetic text about being.

Defending Ancient Springs by Kathleen Raine (essays: Golgonooza Press 1985). Illuminating essays in a spiritual context, including Blake and Shelley, Yeats and David Gascoyne. Available from 3, Cambridge Drive, Ipswich, IP2 9EP.

W.B. Yeats and the Learning of the Imagination by Kathleen Raine (Golgonooza, 1999). Excellent short text, with chapter *'Poetry as Prophecy'*. Available from 3, Cambridge Drive, Ipswich, IP2 9EP

He, and She by Robert A. Johnson (Harper &

Row/HarperSanFrancisco, USA, 1993). Essential and brief reading about the male and female journeys by a noted Jungian analyst.

The Razor's Edge by Somerset Maugham (Pan). Classic novel from the 1930's about a drop-out/mystic called Larry.

A Room of One's Own by Virginia Woolf (Panther Granada). Classic about finding and maintaining one's own space as a writer and as a woman writer.

Journal of a Solitude by May Sarton (Norton, USA). Beautiful descriptions, useful for for own journal work as a model.

The Act of Will by Roberto Assagioli (Turnstone/Penguin). Last work from the founder of psychosynthesis (c. 1975), detailling the stages of the act of will, very useful also in terms of understanding the creative process. Also contact Institute of Psychosynthesis, 65a Watford Way, Hendon, London NW4 (tel: 0208 202 4525).

Sculpting in Time – reflections on the cinema by Andrei Tarkovsky (Bodley Head, 1985). For Ingmar Bergman, Tarkovsky (d. Jan 1987) was *the* director: his poetic films are unique for their atmosphere, now at last available in most decent video/DVD stores.

The Invitation by Oriah Mountain Dreamer (Thorsons, 1999). Commentary about life and living based on her celebrated prose-poem which begins 'It doesn't interest me what you do for a living...'. Also *The Dance* (2001)

Suggested Poetry Journal Subscriptions (recommended)

Acumen edited by Patricia Oxley. Quarterly journal with a broad range of contributors. For info write to Acumen 6, The Mount, Higher Furzenham, Brixham, South Devon TQ5 8QY.

Tears in the Fence Edited by David Caddy. From the founder of The Wessex Festival, this often includes New American Poets as well. For info write to 38, Hod View, Stourpaine, nr Blandford Forum, Dorset DT11 8TN, or email: david@david-caddy.wanadoo.co.uk

Stride an online magazine as well as publishing house, with a more experimental emphasis edited by Rupert M. Loydell. (RML@stridebooks.co.uk).

Information on Poetry Magazines
(with a view to submitting your poems)

You can get an up to date list of poetry magazines and journals from The Poetry Society, (which also produces *Poetry Review*) 22 Betterton Street, Covent Garden, London WC2.

There is also the *Oriel List of Small Publishers & Magazines* edited by Peter Finch (1997) available from the Oriel Bookshop, The Friary, Cardiff.

More up to date is *Light's List* from John Light & Kathy Chamberlin at Photon Press, 37 The Meadows, Berwick-upon-Tweed, Northumberland TD15 1NY

email: photon.press@virgin.net

Libraries
It is always good to get your local library to order poetry books. It's good for you – and for poetry.

The Poetry Library on Level 5 of the South Bank/RFH complex in London (Embankment tube, then walk over the bridge) is well worth a visit. Its collection is comprehensive, as its setting suggests.

REFERENCES

Introduction: References

epigraphs: *'The Dream of the Rood'*, translated by Michael Alexander, from his *The Earliest English Poems* (Penguin).

The lines from Goethe's *'Faust'* from Colin Wilson's *Poetry & Mysticism* (City Lights, USA).

T.S. Eliot's *'The Waste Land'* is published in *Collected Poems* (Faber).

David Gascoyne's concept appears in his *'Prelude to a New Fin De Siecle'* (Greville Press Pamphlets, Emscote Lawn, Warwick). His *Collected Poems* are published by OUP.

Coleridge's *Biographia Literaria* published by J.M. Dent; George Trevelyan's *Magic Casements* by Coventure.

Chapter 1: References

The epigraph to these notes is taken from Kahlil Gibran's *Jesus the Son of Man* (Heinemann).

Rimbaud's *Collected Poems* (which include his letters from which the French quotation is taken) translated by Paul Schmidt & published by Harper Colophon USA. There is also an edition of his poems published by Picador p/b.

Yevtushenko's *The Face Behind The Face* is published by Marion Boyars.

Blake's poem is taken from Selected Poems (Heinemann, ed. F.W.Bateson):

and Kathleen Raine is a leading authority on his work.

e.e. cumming's poem is taken from *The Penguin Book of English Verse* (ed. John Hayward).

Chapter 2 references
The epigraph to these notes is taken from Jung's *The Integration Of The Personality* (Bollingen Foundation series).

The quote from Cicely Berry is taken from her *Voice And The Actor* (Harrap).

The old Wicca saying appears in Starhawk's *Dreaming The Dark* (Beacon Press, USA).

Hardy's poem is taken from *Selected Poems Of Thomas Hardy* (Macmillan's English Classics, ed. P.N.Furbank), which has useful notes at the back.

Michele Robert's poem is taken from *The Mirror Of The Mother* (Methuen).

Akhmatova's poem, translated by Richard McKane, is taken from *Selected Poems* (Bloodaxe Books).

Chapter 3 references
William Arkle was the author of *The Great Gift* (Neville Spearman, 1974), as well as other books and pamphlets in connection with his painting and thought, synthesized in his audiovisual work.

Blaise Pascal's *Pensées* are available in translation (Penguin).

The story about Rumi appears in Darshan 24 (May 1989) in Cynthia Franklin's *'Seeking The Beloved'* (PO Box 600, South

Fallsburg, NY 12779 USA).

For the full story of his life changing meeting with Shams of Tabriz, see Andrew Harvey's *The Way of Passion* (Souvenir Press), and Coleman Barks' *The Essential Rumi* (Penguin), or the novel *Rumi's Daughter*.

John Keats' phrase appears in one of his letters.

Dylan Thomas' poem appears in his *Collected* published by Dent; Brian Patten's in Love Poems (Allen & Unwin).

Old Chinese saying, attributed to Chuang Tzu: 'A thousand mile journey begins with the first step'.

Emily Dickinson's poem is taken from *Love: A Keepsake* (Unirose), and appears in her Collected published by Faber.

D.H.Lawrence's poem is taken from *Selected Poems*, ed. Keith Sagar (Penguin).

W.H.Davies' poem is taken from The Oxford Book of English Verse ed. Philip Larkin (Oxford University Press).

Kenneth Patchen *Love Poems* (New Directions, USA).

Elaine Randell's poem is taken from *Transformation the poetry of spiritual consciousness* ed. by the present author (Rivelin Grapheme Press, 1988). Some copies still available from CHRYSALIS (see Further Information).

Owen Davis I+I (Rivelin Grapheme Press, The Annexe, Kennet House, 19 Church St, Hungerford, Berks RG17 ONL £4.95 (his section *'The Burning Performer'*)

Elaine Randell *Beyond All Other* (Pig Press).

Chapter 4 References

Mysticism, edited and introduced by F.C.Happold (Penguin) which contains a very useful introduction (*'The Study'*) with a particularly clear evocation of *'The Timeless Moment'*. The section on Richard Jefferies is very relevant here too.

Wordsworth's *'Tintern Abbey'* is available most editions of his poems.

Kim Taplin *Tongues In Trees* (Green Books, 1989) is available from Resurgence, Ford House, Hartland, Bideford, North Devon EX39 6EE It. also has a very good chapter on Richard Jeffries.

Paul Matthews' poem is taken from *Transformation* (as before, 1988).
It also appears in *Two Stones One Bird* (with Owen Davis) published by The Poetry Business; and in *The Ground that Love Seeks* (Five Seasons Press) available direct from the author; contact Paul Matthews c/o Emerson College, Forest Row, Sussex, RH18 5JX

Paul Matthews *The Fabulous Names Of Things* and *The Ground that Love Seeks*, is available from him c/o Emerson College as above @ £10 inclusive of postage.

John Keats, in his letters.

Gerard Manley Hopkins' poems are available from Penguin; and there is a chapter on him (*'Bats'*) in Jeremy Reed's *Madness The Price Of Poetry* (Peter Owen).

Gason Bachelard's books are published in translation by Beacon Press, Boston, USA and include specific to these notes *The Poetics Of Space*, and his last work, *The Poetics Of Reverie*.

Francis Ponge has been translated in *Things*, available from The Poetry Library, Level 5, South Bank Centre, London, SW1.

Neruda's poems are published (in translation from the Spanish) by Penguin in UK and Grove Press (53 East 11th St New York NY 10003) in America.

The quote, from *'Towards An Impure Poetry'* is taken from *Five Decades: Poems 19251970*, which is the Grove Press 'Evergreen' edition.

MacLeish's poem is taken from the updated *Palgrave's Golden Treasury*.

Ted Hughes' poem is taken from *Moortown* (Faber, 1979).

Chapter 5 References

Novalis *Hymns To The Night*, translated by David Gascoyne and Jeremy Reed (Enitharmon Press, 40 Rushes Road, Petersfield, Hants)

The quotation from Novalis, translated by Charles E. Passage, appears in Robert Bly's anthology *News Of The Universe - poems of twofold consciousness* (Sierra Club Books, 1980).

This anthology is also available via Green Books, Ford House, Hartland, Bideford, North Devon EX39 6EE in a reprinted edition.

Bly's remarks about energy appear in *'A Meditation On A Poem By Yeats'*, as an afterword to that anthology.

The quotation from Peter Redgrove is taken from *'The Voice Of*

Peter Redgrove' in *The Third Eye* ('the psychic issue' / April 1984 edited by the present author).

For information about contemporary Druidry, see the course offered by O.B.O.D. (Order Of Bards, Ovates and Druids) at PO Box 1333 Lewes, East Sussex BN7 1DX. Email: office@druidry.org

Mary Shelley's *Frankenstein* was a success far beyond her expectations, which came to symbolize the European shadow. The book is easily available.

Keats' famous passage about 'Soulmaking' appears in his letter to George & Georgiana Keats, written in February 1819. Shelley's quote also appears in a letter; there is also his equally relevant *A Defence Of Poetry*, written around the same time.

Rilke's *Letters To A Young Poet*, translated by M.D. Herter Norton, (published by W.W.Norton & Co., 500 Fifth Avenue, New York, N.Y. 10110 USA and 37 Great Russell St, London WCIB 3NU).

Herman Hesse's poem is taken from Robert Bly's *News From The Universe* (Green Books), translated by him.

Sylvia Plath's poem is taken from *Collected Poems*, ed. Ted Hughes (Faber).

Robert Bly's poem is taken from *Loving A Woman In Two Worlds* (Harper & Row, USA).

'Trust the process' was advice given to me by Bronwen Astor; and 'All you need to do to write...' in conversation with Joan Evans of the London Institute of Psychosynthesis, now based in Hendon & Mill Hill.

Transformation, ed. by the present author and available from CHRYSALIS.

Into the Further Reaches – an anthology of Contemporary British Poetry celebrating the spiritual journey (ed. Jay Ramsay, PS Avalon, 2007) available from www.psavalon.com or 27, Roman Way, Glastonbury, Somerset BA6 8YR.

Chapter 6 References

The epigraph to these notes is taken from T.S. Eliot's *'Little Gidding'* (*Four Quartets*) published by Faber. Eliot's *'Journey Of The Magi'* is in his Faber *Collected Poems*.

Shelley's *Alastor* dates from 1815, written when he was twenty three. Shelley's poem is taken from *Poetical Works* ed. By Thomas Hutchinson (OUP), who also published the 1946 edition I have of H.D.'s *The Flowering Of The Rod*.

Bunyan's *Pilgrim's Progress* is easily available.

The Arthurian material is available via numerous sources: traditionally, Thomas Malory's *Morte D'Arthur*, and through Chretien de Troyes (France).

There is an Everyman hardback edition of his *Arthurian Romances* in translation.

Interpretations can be found in Edward C. Whitmont's *The Return Of The Goddess* (Arkana p/b),

Robert A. Johnson's *He* (Harper & Row, USA) which tells the story of Parsifal and Emma Jung / Marie Louise von Frantz's classic *The Grail Legend*, a must for in-depth appreciation.

A.L. Hendriks' poem is in *To Speak Simply* (Hippopotamus Press, 1989); and extracted from in *Transformation* (ed. Jay Ramsay).
Danté meets Virgil in a dark wood at the beginning of *The Divine*

Comedy.
A good translation is C.H. Sisson's, published by Pan p/b.

Creeley's *Hello: A Journal* is published by Marion Boyars (1978). It's a medley of short or 'minimalist' poems written on a journey he made through South East Asia.

Frances Horovitz's poem is taken from her *Collected Poems* ed. Roger Garfitt, (published by Bloodaxe).

Journey to Eden by Jenny Davis and Jay Ramsay (Eden Centre Books), is available from Jenny Davis at 5, Old Farm, Manstone Lane, Sidmouth, S. Devon EX10 9TX @ £7.50 inclusive of p&p.

Chapter 7 References
The phrase from Dante is the last line of his *Paradiso*.

Auden's poem is taken from *Collected Shorter Poems* 1927-1957 (Faber);

Gascoyne's is from *Collected Poems* (Oxford: reprinted by Penguin);

Ted Hughes' from *Moortown* (Faber see previous notes); and Gabriel Bradford Millar's (Lanny Kennish) and Pippa Little's from *Transformation* (ed. Jay Ramsay).

Angels Of Fire - an anthology of radical poetry in the '80's, edited by the present author with Sylvia Paster and Jeremy Silver (Chatto & Windus, 1986); and *Transformation* (ed. Jay Ramsay), as cited.

Gabriel Bradford Millar (nee Lanny Kennish)'s *The Saving Flame* (Five Seasons Press), a selection of poems over 25 years, is available from her at The Studio, The Lindens, Lower St, Stroud, Glos. for £10.

She also appears with a significant group of 'journeying poets' in *Into the Further Reaches – an anthology of Contemporary British Poetry celebrating the spiritual journey* (ed. Jay Ramsay, PSAvalon, 2007) from www.psavalon.com or 27, Roman Way, Glastonbury, Somerset BA6 8YR for £15 inclusive of p&p.

Angels Of Fire - an anthology of radical poetry in the '80's, edited by Jay Ramsay with Sylvia Paster and Jeremy Silver (Chatto & Windus, 1986);

Christopher Smart was a contemporary of William Blake's. His poems are published by Carcanet.

Susan Hill's *The Bird of Night* is published by Penguin.
Jeremy Reed's *Madness, the price of Poetry* is published by Peter Owen.
Kenneth Patchen's *The Journal of Albion Moonlight* is published by New Directions, USA.

Ezra Pound's *The Cantos* is published, also in extracted form, by Faber.
    Larkin, utterly different as he is, also.

The quotation from Alan Jackson is taken from *Salutations, Collected Poems*, 1960-1989 (Polygon Press, Edinburgh), *Heart Of The Sun* is published by Open Township (14, Foster Clough, Heights Road, Hebdenbridge, W.Yorks.). Enquiries also to the author at 40, Angle Park Terrace, Edinburgh, EH11 2PJ (alan45jax@beeb.net).

Matthew Fox's *Meditations with Meister Eckhart* (Bear & Co, Santa Fe, New Mexico).

Enid Starkie's biography of Rimbaud.

Chapter 8 References

Virginia Woolf's *A Room Of One's Own* is published by Panther Granada.

The Enemies Of Promise is available in many libraries.

John Fairfax was the poetry editor of *Resurgence* before Glenn Storhaug, and subsequently Peter Abbs. His books, including *Wild Children*, are published by Phoenix Press (The Thatched Cottage, Eling, Hermitage, nr. Newbury, Berks RG16 9XR).

The biblical reference is to Psalm 40 ('I waited, I waited on the Lord').

No marks for guessing who wrote *Othello*. For anyone interested in the philosophy of being, see also the writings of Martin Heidegger (his concept of *Dasein*).

Paterson is published by New Directions (see last chapter's notes ref. Patchen).

Arseny Tarkovsky's poem is taken from Andrei Tarkovsky's *Sculpting In Time* (Bodley Head). Arseny and Andrei were father and son. Andrei died in Paris in 1986, and his extraordinary poetic films are worth going a long way to see.

Rosemary Palmeira's poem is taken from *Transformation*. She was the editor of *In The Gold Of Flesh - poems of birth & motherhood* (Women's Press, 1990), which is itself a meditation on creativity.

Rainer Maria Rilke's 'The One Birds Plunge Through' is in Selected Poems, translated by Leisham (Penguin), as quoted.

Edwin Muir's 'Nothing There But Faith' is in his *Collected*, published by Faber.

Susan Hill's *The Magic Apple Tree* (Bodley Head);

Piero Ferruci's *What We May Be - the visions and techniques of Psychosynthesis* (Turnstone Press/Penguin).

For further reference to the Will, see Roberto Assagioli's *The Act Of Will* (Turnstone Press/ Penguin). Assagioli was the founder of Psychosynthesis, having been associated as a young man with Jung. For further information about Psychosynthesis and one-to-one sessions, please see Further Information.

Prospero's Cell is published by Faber. Lawrence Durrell died in the South of France in 1990. 'Kalamai' is now called Kalami Bay. The White House still stands, and you can eat and stay there.

For more remote Greek islands (like Hydra), and renting individual villas, I would recommend Twelve Islands. They are based in Romford, Essex and their prices are competitive. See also www.rosyslittlevillage.com which is on Agistri.

For remote places in Britain, such as Rosemerryn Wood in Cornwall, set in woods with a fougou, you can consult the back pages of magazines such as *Resurgence, Caduceus, Kindred Spirit* and *The Spark*. For a list of ecumenical retreats see The Vision, published annually.

Places To Be edited by Jonathan How (Coherent Visions, 2002) is a guidebook of retreats. See info@places-to-be.com

Chapter 9 References

The Observer's Book Of Butterflies, compiled by W.J. Stokoe, is published by Frederick Warne & Co. (1973).

Quotations in these notes are from 'The Life Cycle Of A Butterfly' p.1531.

Gillian Allnutt's *Spitting out the pips* is published by Sheba

Feminist Publishers, 488 Kingsland Road, London E8. See also her Blackthorn (Bloodaxe).

'Some poems read like ice': see Geoffrey Hill's *Tenebrae* (Andre Deutsch)

The lines from Eliot are taken from *'Burnt Norton'* in *Four Quartets* (Faber).

re: D.H. Lawrence, see his medley *'The Ship Of Death'*. There is a recent very large *Collected* ed. Keith Sagar, published by Penguin.

Matthew Fox's *Original Blessing* (Bear & Co., Santa Fe, New Mexico) This is an invigorating interpretation of Eckhart's fourfold path see *'The Journey Of Poets'* and I refer you particularly to the third section, Themes 16-20, on the *'Via Creativa'* which has to do with creativity and resurrection, and the figure of Christ as a poet... as I began by quoting, out of Kahlil Gibran.

Quotations from interviews with contemporary poets taken from the poetry journal *Acumen* edited by Patricia Oxley. Issue 10 includes an interview with Jay Ramsay (Dec. 1988). Contact: The Mount, Higher Furzenham, Brixham, South Devon TQ5 8QY.

IF YOU WISH TO WORK WITH A TUTOR/GUIDE

If you wish to work with me or one of my experienced poetry colleagues, please apply in writing giving your name, address and phone details to: *The Poet in You*, 5 Oxford Terrace, Uplands, Stroud, Glos. GL5 1TW. Please also include your email address.

You will be invited to simply write in with feedback from the exercises in each chapter, taking each chapter as a month period. You are also invited to send in written work, and (where indicated) comments on the study poems.

Each letter of yours will be responded to once a month, making up 9 letters in all in correspondence.

The course fee is £180 for 9 months. Cheques are payable to CHRYSALIS, please. Payments are requested in advance.

In addition, there is a continuation of this course for a further 9 months, with 9 sets of notes, which you can also apply for. The fee is £200, inclusive of cost of materials.

This also operates by correspondence, with exercises and written work to be sent in, as before.

FURTHER INFORMATION

There are regular monthly poetry group gatherings in both London at The Lotus Foundation (nr. Swiss Cottage) and Gloucestershire (near Nailsworth) run by Jay Ramsay. Evenings combine creative meditation with writing and constructive critical group feedback.

Further information from www.lotusfoundation.org.uk (Genie Poretsky-Lee/0207-794-8880) – and Maxine Relton on 01453-832597. Also from 01453-759436.

There are also regular poetry weekends and day workshops at Hawkwood College, Stroud (01453-759034): 'Chrysalis 1.' (The Sacred Space of the Word – end of February), 'Chrysalis 2. (Keeping the Faith – November/December), as well as 'The Poet in You' (October/November), and 'Edges'.

Chrysalis also organizes summer residential retreats, here and abroad, which combine poetry with personal development, art and dance. Please let us know of your interest: in writing to 5, Oxford Terrace, Uplands, Stroud, Glos GL5 1TW or by phone (01453-759436). Please also include your email address.

A full list of Jay Ramsay's available publications (and CD recordings) is also available on request.

ACKNOWLEDGEMENTS

Some of the Preface 'From Chrysalis to Butterfly' was first published in *Network Ireland* and also *Lapidus, Touchstone, Healing Today, South West Connection* and *Gloucestershire Connections*. My thanks to those editors.

Special thanks to Carole Bruce, who gave me the idea to develop my teaching in this form in what became the two 9 month courses which comprise *Chrysalis – the poet in you*, originally composed through 1990-1991 in Kew, London; and near Painswick, Stroud, Gloucestershire. Also to Philip Carr-Gomm for his early encouragement while he was developing O.B.O.D. a few streets away in Kew.

Thanks also to Jenny Davis, Ken Davis, and Jeannie Karr (then in Lynton, North Devon) for their wonderful support, also in first putting all the notes on computer disk during 1991-2. Thanks also to Carolyn Finlay (1993-4), and Roselle Angwin (1998-9) for working with my Part 1 students so engagingly. Also to Anne Jorgensen (2002-3) for encouraging me to find a publisher.

Thanks also to all the various centre administrators and friends who have supported my work with poetry and personal development; especially Chrysalis in Donard, Co. Wicklow, Ireland (1992-4), and Hawkwood College near Stroud, Gloucestershire (since 1993); also Rosemary Palmeira and Alec Taylor in Portugal, Marlene Saliba in Malta, Fiona Owen in Anglesey, Catherine Leonard in Co. Dublin, Ruth Marshall in Co. Clare (*Network Ireland*), and Claire Knifton-Russell in Co. Sligo, Ireland.

Warm thanks to John Hunt at O Books for his faith in the material, and his willingness to accept it in unabridged form. Poetry, perhaps, is the one thing that cannot be dumbed down !

And finally, thanks to all my many students past and present who go on making the work feel so essentially worthwhile.

J.R.